The Complete Guide to Meeting Men and Finding Mr. Right

by Don Diebel

I0157364

Copyright 2023 by Don Diebel

Gemini Publishing Company
818 Lois Street, Suite A
Kerrville, TX 78028
Website: http://www.getgirls.com

ISBN 9780937164419

Table of Contents

INTRODUCTION

This book offers proven and practical solutions for the overwhelming number of women who face the very real problem of meeting men and finding Mr. Right.

I wrote this book on the basis of three underlying principles:

First, using the law of probabilities. If you make it your goal to constantly go where and be where many men congregate, and if you put all your efforts into trying to meet as many men as possible, you will sooner or later meet a man who will fulfill all your dreams. A man capable of intimacy, not afraid of commitment, communicates, and will fall in love with you exactly as you are.

As you read, "The Complete Guide to Meeting Men and Finding Mr. Right," you're going to be amazed at the many ways, methods, and techniques to meet men.

Try as many methods as possible. Don't put all your eggs in one basket. A good example of this is women who only go to nightclubs to meet men. Date many men and date often! Set a goal to meet and go out with a hundred men. Long before you have met your one hundredth man, in most cases, you will have found at least one, but more probably, many men who will be right for you.

To sum it up, you need exposure and visibility. One of the major reasons you may not be finding a special man is simply because you're not meeting enough men.

The second principle is based upon women's inability to make the first move because of shyness, fear of rejection, and thinking that the man must make the first move. This book will teach you to go after what you want and become aggressive. Believe me; men want you to make the first move.

Today the choice is all yours. Either you can sit around waiting for men to approach you...or use the surefire techniques in this book to take control of your love-life once and for all.

Now, after reading this book you can actually go up to any man and let him know you're interested in him and have exactly the kind of relationship you're looking for. Your social power becomes almost limitless.

You've got to take action to get the things you want out of life! Don't sit around waiting for "the man of your dreams"to come into your life. If you leave the business of finding love with the right man to chance, chances are it will pass you by.

Sure, this is going to involve some risk-taking and courage to be aggressive in meeting men. With practice, it will come natural and besides, this is an investment in your future happiness.

The last principle this book is based on is using the powers of the subconscious mind to meet men and reprogram your mind with positive thoughts and eliminate the negative "garbage" in your subconscious mind that causes you problems with the opposite sex.

You may be a little skeptical of some of these methods to reprogram your mind to meet men, overcome shyness, gain confidence with men, etc. These proven scientific methods are guaranteed to work and will work for you if you back them with desire and belief. With practice, you will be meeting more men than you ever dreamed possible!

In closing, make finding "the man of your dreams" your top priority in life. Set goals and become obsessed with attracting him.

I've designed a personal game plan for you to meet men that work. The rest is up to you. *Happy Hunting!*

Chapter 1 - How to Meet Men in Nightclubs

Where's one of the best places in your city to meet a man? You guessed it right. A nightclub. This is where men go to unwind and release their pent-up pressures and emotions, not to mention, meeting a woman like yourself. The clubs provide an atmosphere of sensual stimulation with all the music, lights, pulsating rhythms, and the erotic and exotic motions of women thrusting their hips to and fro.

There's an art to meeting men in clubs and this book will lead you and guide you from the moment you walk in the door until the time you leave. You'll learn how to approach men and what to do after you have made contact.

If you're a shy woman, reading this book will give you the confidence and the ability to meet men at the clubs. Using the methods in this book, your fear of the opposite sex will disappear and you won't be standing on the sidelines anymore watching the other women meet men.

You may be a little skeptical of some of the methods used to meet men in this book. These methods will work for any woman that employs them backed with desire and belief. If you don't believe they will work for you, just try them out for yourself and you will be amazed at the results. With practice, you will be meeting more men than you ever dreamed possible.

Let's not waste anymore time talking about what you're going to learn and get down to business and "make it" with the nightclub man.

How to Select a Good Club

When selecting a club, you want to select one where most of the men are. To do this, you can try and hit as many clubs as possible and check out the action for yourself or you can ask your friends that frequent the nightclub scene. However, what they consider a great place to meet men may not necessarily be the best place to go. You might also ask the door man upon arriving, what's the best night for action. Also, while you're there, inquire if they have a ladies night when ladies drink free or get a discount on their drinks. So, don't stay home when there's a ladies night!

When shopping around for a club, don't make the fatal mistake of judging a club on the basis of one night. Certain nights can just be an off night. This is normal and happens at all clubs.

Don't waste your time going to a club where there are mostly women. The more men there are, the chances are greatly increased of you meeting someone.

You may want to select an exclusive membership club if you can afford it. Just make it a point to take an introductory tour. Sometimes it's free or you pay a cover charge to check it out.

Conventional clubs are just as good, if not better. The majority of people might not be upper-class and rich but this will be to your advantage and I will explain why. An upper-class, high society jet-setter nightclub man is usually narcissistic and self-centered and if you don't have money you're just scum of the earth. There are exceptions to the rule, however.

Your conventional club is your best bet in my opinion. Here you will find a variety of men, the successful and barely-making-it, attractive men, blue collar men, professional men, and your average "Plain Joe."

They all have the same thing in common and that is to get out on that dance floor and shed their inhibitions and most important of all, to meet a woman like yourself.

In conclusion, find a nightclub where the greatest number of men are and that you feel comfortable in and keep going there as often as possible. Make an effort to meet as many people as possible, including other women. After all, women know men and they can introduce you to their male friends, relatives, and co-workers. By going to this place often, you will become a familiar face and you will be amazed at the number of friends and acquaintances you will make. So get out there and make the rounds and find yourself a good nightclub. Just keep going to this nightclub and see if your social life doesn't improve dramatically.

Also, I might add, don't just go to a few nightclubs when selecting a nightclub. Go to all of them so you can make a good comparison as to which ones are the best. Some nightclubs are good only on a particular night. Find out what night that is and make an effort to be there every week.

I know you have heard various comments in books, media, etc. about nightclubs being one of the worst places to look for a relationship or a husband. A lot of my female friends have met real nice men and had satisfying relationships with men they have met in nightclubs.

So, don't rule out nightclubs as good places to meet men. Try several different methods of meeting men. Don't put all your eggs in one basket and use nightclubs solely for the purpose of meeting the opposite sex.

Some women make the fatal mistake of carrying a negative attitude with them when they go to nightclubs. They think that all the men there are just a bunch of bastards. This attitude can prevent you from meeting someone really nice. There are some really nice men in nightclubs that will treat you with respect. Also, a lot of men are looking for a special woman to love.

The Nightclub Man

I will describe the different types of men you will encounter at the nightclubs.

First, I will begin with the undesirable types which should be avoided if at all possible, because you will just be wasting your time. Believe me, you don't want to waste your precious time trying to meet a man you're not going to get anywhere with. Before you know it, closing time will creep upon you and you will say to yourself, "I wasted my whole damn night on that man and here I am going home alone without at least getting his phone number."

The following are what I classify as the undesirable types:

The Woman Hater

Why in the hell these men go to nightclubs I'll never be able to figure out. Because of some negative experiences with the opposite sex and because they have been hurt, they think all women are bitches. These men will just sit there with a stone face, rejecting any glances from the opposite sex. If you approach them and try to start up a conversation, they give you a go to hell look that says, "Go away bitch."

No matter what approach you use, how attractive you are, or how friendly you act, you will be rejected. A lot of these men subconsciously gain immense pleasure out of putting women down. Some will even tell you to go to hell or get lost if you ask them to dance or just by trying to start up a conversation with them.

I'm just glad this type of put down does not happen very often. Usually, men do not object to a woman approaching them if it is done properly.

If you run into this type of man, whatever you do, DON'T try to get even with him by putting him down and showing anger towards him. He loves that and there is nothing he would like better than to see you get bent out of shape. By making you unhappy, it makes him happy to see women suffer.

Simply ignore his rejection towards you and move on to the next available man that catches your eye. Fortunately, you will not run into many men like this. There are plenty of men who want to meet and mingle with women.

The Teaser

Unfortunately you will run into these types at the nightclubs and in all areas of life. You have seen them in high school, college, at work, strip joints, etc. Just learn to recognize them and ignore and avoid them. I will give you some tips on how to spot them:

1. He wears very revealing clothes. He wears very tight clothes showing off his muscles and perhaps the bulge in his crotch. Also, the non-teaser wears these kinds of clothes to attract a woman's attention, but the teaser wears them with the attitude of, "You can look but you better not touch." The minute you try to get physical with him or try to make advances toward him, he gives you the big brush off. Showing off his body is just to attract attention and nothing else.

2. While dancing he looks more like a male stripper, thrusting his hips back and forth and shaking his crotch at you. He's doing this on purpose to turn you on and fool you into thinking he's an easy catch. The song ends and he says, "Thank you" and disappears into the crowd. Before you know it he's back up on the dance floor with another woman doing the same thing to her. He will do this with several women, never spending much time with any particular woman. He gets his thrills by turning on as many women as possible on the dance floor, but has no intentions whatsoever of getting picked up or meeting anyone.

3. Here's one that really bothers you. You see this really hot and sexy man flirting with you and really giving you the eye. You try to meet this man and he tells you, "I've got to go to the restroom" and then he never returns. Another one is, "I've got to go look for my friend" and never returns. Later you see him in another part of the nightclub. He deliberately leaves the scene to avoid making any contact with any woman, much less you.

4. This will really frustrate you. You ask this man to slow dance and he accepts. Your bodies meet and he starts grinding his crotch into yours. You're getting turned on and horny. All this time you're thinking he's horny too and wants to make love to you. The song ends and he abruptly breaks away and says, "Thank you" and then disappears into the crowd. Then you say in your mind, "That damned teaser!"

5. This is known as a big flirt. He walks around flirting with every woman in sight. When a woman approaches him trying to make

contact, he rejects her advances or makes up an excuse to leave the scene.

6. This experience can really blow your mind. You meet a man and you drink and dance the night away. You think you're really hitting it off well together and you get the impression he will go home with you. You ask him if he would like to come over to your place for a while. He says, "No" and you ask him if he would like to leave and get a bite to eat at a local restaurant. He still says, "No." So you say, "Well can I give you a call sometime?" He replies, "I don't give out my phone number to strangers." So it ends up that you wasted your whole night on this one.

The Drinkaholic

This is a man who uses women to support a drinking habit. He may even come right out and ask you, "Would you buy me a drink?" upon meeting you. Most women will not buy a man a drink, but if you do, after he finishes his drink he will say, "Can I have another drink?" One drink leads to another and before you know it, you have dished out a lot of money on his drinks.

This all can surely be to your advantage or disadvantage. On the positive side, he may go home with you in exchange for buying him drinks. He may get so drunk it may be necessary to take him home and put him to bed. Of course on the negative side he may just use you to buy him drinks and then blow you off and leave the nightclub or even move on to the next fool who will buy him drinks.

In conclusion, use your better judgment before you start dishing out a lot of money on buying a man drinks. You could be taken for a ride. Fortunately, you will very rarely run into this type of man.

The (Dance Only) Man

This is the man that goes to the nightclub to dance only. He's not going there to be hustled, attract women or go home with anybody. He just wants to dance and have a good time.

In some cases he might be married or going out on his girlfriend. This would explain why he would just want to dance, with no strings attached, that is if he wants to remain faithful.

Although this type may be undesirable initially because of his reluctance to be approached, don't give up on him. The next night you see him, dance with him again as many times as possible. After you practically become dancing partners, you will become more and more acquainted with each other and before you know it he will have other things on his mind besides dancing.

Out With the Boys Night

These are groups of men who come to the nightclubs to socialize among themselves. They may be all single, married, or both. They came to the nightclub to have a few drinks and shoot the bull. Some just want to socialize among themselves and don't want to be bothered by any women.

It's rather difficult to meet men who are in a group like this, much less make contact. Some of them may dance, but after the dance they go rushing back to their male friends and just ignore you. If you can determine if a man is part of a group like this and he ignores you and seems like he's just interested in his friends, don't waste your time and move on to greener pastures.

If you find out he's married and with a group of married men, you're really at a dead end street. They should not even be there in the first place. I strongly recommend not having anything to do with a married man at a nightclub. What if his wife walks in the nightclub and sees his husband with another woman? This can only spell trouble. Let me warn you and take my advice, STAY AWAY FROM MARRIED MEN!

The Gold-digger Man

This man is mainly interested in how much material wealth and money you have. Upon meeting you, he will ask personal questions like, "What do you do for a living?", "How much money do you make?", "What kind of car do you drive?", "Do you own your own home?", or "Do you have a boat?"

If you're not a woman of financial means, he may not have anything to do with you. He will consider you too low-classed to associate with. If you are a woman of financial means, then you will probably hit it off real well with this type of man. This can have its drawbacks though, because he may just like you for your money and not for yourself.

This concludes the undesirable types. Now I will describe the desirable types you will encounter at the nightclubs:

The Woman-Hunter

This man goes to nightclubs with one purpose in mind. To meet women and get approached by you. This is one of the easiest types to meet because there are no hassles involved. You meet, have a couple drinks and dance, and he's ready and willing to pursue the relationship further and he may even go home with you. He may come right out and tell you, "I want to make love to you" (don't get your hopes up on this one, it's very unlikely) or "Let's leave and go to your place." An aggressive man may scare some women off but don't let it bother you. Admire a man having courage to go for what he wants.

Some of these men may be very active sexually and like to play musical sex partners. They need sex constantly and with a variety of sexual partners. It may be nice to meet a man like this sometimes, but most likely it will turn into a one-nighter. He wakes up the next day and gets dressed and walks right out of your life.

One possible drawback from meeting a sexually active man like this is contracting a social disease. Of course, how are you supposed to know he has been sleeping with lots of women in the city. You just have to be careful who you sleep with these days.

These types are usually easy to spot. They actively flirt and smile at the opposite sex and are extremely friendly. They will just stand around the dance floor where they encourage women to ask them to dance. They, of course, may ask you to dance. I really admire a man who takes the initiative to ask a woman to dance. Some men are so shy about asking a woman to dance in the first place.

Also, I might add, these men usually come to the nightclubs alone. However, they come with a girlfriend occasionally. A man alone will get approached more often by women. So, for the Man-Hunter, it's really an advantage for him to go to the nightclubs alone so he will be approached more frequently.

The High and Loaded Man

This is a man who is either high on liquor or drugs or even both. After a few drinks or under the influence of drugs, he will be feeling rather loose and perhaps even horny. Naturally, this is to your advantage because it makes your prey easier to catch.

How do you spot this man? By simple observation. His walk will be unsteady, while perhaps bumping into people while he is walking. If he has been drinking heavily, he will make several trips to the restroom. By standing next to the men's restroom, you can observe who's going back and forth to the restroom. An exception to this is a man that has a kidney or bladder problem.

If he's under the influence of drugs, his pupils will be very large. If he's loaded on downers, he will walk as if he were drunk and his speech will be somewhat slurred.

Don't come on real strong and act real aggressive with this man. He possibly may think that you are trying to take advantage of him because he's loaded. Just be nice and gentle with him.

The Mate-Seeker

This is a man who is actively seeking a lover or girlfriend. He's unattached and looking for a relationship. Perhaps in the back of his mind he wants to settle down and get married.

Unfortunately, a nightclub is not the best place in the world to look for a long-term relationship or marriage partner. A lot of men are just out to see how many different women they can make love to and don't want to be tied down to any serious relationships. They have a love them and leave them attitude. The same thing applies to some women who frequent nightclubs.

This type of man is highly desirable because he's very friendly and easy to make contact with. You can make a very strong impression on this man by showing him that you're interested in him and care for him. You shouldn't have any problem getting him to leave to get something to eat or go home with you, if you play your cards right.

The Rich Man

He is usually dressed in expensive clothes and perhaps wears a lot of gold and diamonds. He may be a bit on the snobbish side because he thinks he's better than everyone else. If you are on the same level as this man and well-to-do yourself, you will probably score points with this man. However, if you are not well-dressed, dignified, and have a low income, you probably won't even get to first base with this man. It's really sad that some men just can't accept you as you are.

There's a way around this if you want to do some acting and lying. You can look rich and act rich even though you are not rich. People are judged first by their appearance. All you have got to do is wear the latest expensive-looking fashions for women and be well groomed. Also, you will probably have to do some lying about your wealth. If you think you can play this role to mingle with rich men, give it a try. Some women will try anything, including lying, to attract a man.

The Shy Man

Just like there are many shy women at nightclubs, there are just as many shy men. The shy man is easy to spot. Shy men will tend to sit where they won't be noticed, like in the corner or in the back of the club, away from all the prowling females.

Some are even too shy to dance, so if you ask this man to dance and he says no, it may just be because he's too shy to dance and not because he's rejecting you. In this case, try to strike up a conversation with him. If this fails, move on.

This man will show his shyness in various ways. Below are just a few examples:

1. While talking to you, his eyes will glance off to the side or down towards the floor. Shy men have difficulty looking at a woman in the eyes while talking to her.
2. He may be lacking in conversational skills. He may be rather quiet, speaking in a low voice and not have very much to say. In this case, you will just have to pick up the slack and do most of the talking yourself.
3. If he has a nice body, he may try to conceal it by wearing clothes that don't compliment his body.
4. Upon meeting him, he will act very nervous. He may tap his fingers on the top of the table or he may tap his feet. He might even bite his nails.
5. While talking, he may stutter quite frequently.
6. When you pay him a compliment, he blushes or does not agree with your compliment.

In conclusion, don't pass up an opportunity to attract or meet a shy man. Once you break the ice and get them warmed up, they can make your night worthwhile.

The Egotist

Unfortunately, these types of people exist in all phases of life and you will see your share of them in the nightclubs.

This man is a stuck up snob and thinks he's hot stuff. He walks around the club with his nose up in the air. If you try to stop him and talk to him, he just ignores you and keeps on walking. This is very annoying to us women. It wouldn't hurt him to be friendly and talk to you. Also, out on the dance floor he will be constantly looking at himself in the mirrors, if there happen to be mirrors on the dance floor. He loves looking at himself.

The egotists are difficult to approach because they think they are too good for you. Don't let this discourage you though. At least make an attempt to meet him and if you fail, there are usually plenty of friendly men to meet. Myself, I'll take a friendly man over a snob any day.

The Nightclub Regulars

These are the men that you'll see time and time again at the nightclubs. They are what I call "regulars." Their whole life revolves around the nightclubs. You can find them at the clubs two or three times during the weeknights and just about every weekend.

Some of these men rarely date. Their whole social life is at the nightclubs with their friends. If he belongs to his own little group of friends, it may be difficult to meet this man. He may just associate and dance with his friends only and consider you an intruder.

If you do determine that a man is a regular, just don't let this discourage you. He can be met just as easily as any other man. The key to getting in good with this man is becoming a regular yourself. This has numerous advantages because you'll become a familiar face to the other regular men. Just keep going to the nightclubs as much as possible and make it a point to meet and mingle with the men you see there regularly.

After going to a particular club regularly, it will be easy to spot the male regulars. When you become a regular yourself, you'll get to know these men on a physical and intimate basis.

The Nightclub EgoWoman

I will describe what I call the "Nightclub Ego Woman" that you will run into at nightclubs. If you're one of these women, resolve here and now that you're going to change your ways and discontinue being the Nightclub Ego-Woman.

This is the woman you will see standing around, depending on her looks to meet men. She may be very attractive or she just thinks she is. She just stands around all night thinking that she's God's gift to men and she waits for men to approach her. She keeps on waiting and waiting, never making the effort or going out of her way to approach and meet men. I don't need to tell you that this type of woman is not very successful at meeting or attracting men.

Believe me; you can't depend on your looks to meet men. It just does not work that way. You have got to approach men and play the aggressor. You can stand around all night and most likely no man is going to approach you and start up a conversation or ask you to dance. You have got to take the lead. I will agree that there are aggressive men who will approach a woman. I just wish there were more of them because I love being approached by a man.

You'll meet as many men as you want by just being friendly and taking the initiative to meet them. It's really just that simple, so don't go walking around with your nose up in the air thinking you are so good-looking that men will literally fall over you.

What to Wear

Now we come to clothes. This can make you or break you and is very important. Clothes do make the woman you know. Nothing will turn off a man more if you are dressed like a slob. Of course, if he's a slob too, he won't care. A decent man admires a woman that is well-groomed and well dressed. Here are some do's and don'ts of nightclub dressing:

1. Whatever you do, don't wear a T-shirt with an offensive slogan on it.

2. Try and wear lightweight material that is cool and not too tight. You're really going to perspire out there on the dance floor and you will feel very uncomfortable if you have got on something hot and heavy.

3. Avoid wearing any clothes with glitter material. This is out!

4. You can get some fashion ideas by watching TV and from Cosmopolitan Magazine.

5. While you're in nightclubs, look around at the other women and you can get some fashion ideas from them.

Try to select way-out or unusual, unique outfits. These will immediately catch the eye of men. By wearing an unusual and unique outfit and being among people in ordinary clothes, you will find yourself to be the center of attention. This is what you want to do and that is, attract a man's attention.

Try to select sexy-looking clothes. By wearing sexy-looking clothes, you will be sending out a message. The message being that you yourself are also sexually stimulating.

Selection of eye-catching colors is very important in attracting attention. The human eye notices color and form simultaneously. If both your colors and form are unusual, strong, and simple, the human eye must take notice of them. The impression will be strong and quick.

Don't go to extremes though, in your selection of clothes and color. Wearing weird clothes that have too strong and conflicting colors will have the opposite effect in attracting attention. You will repel and you will be labeled as some kind of "weirdo."

One last item on dressing that really turns on and attracts men. When buying clothes, buy them tight-fitting,

It's a known fact that men also look at a woman's body just like we look at a man's body. So, why not give them something to drool over.

Getting Ready and Psyched Up

Psyching yourself up and making preparations before going to a nightclub are very important. Be sure and get a good night's sleep before you go out. At least seven to eight hours will be sufficient. Eat a good steak dinner with your choice of vegetables prior to going out. This will put a lining on your stomach if you do a lot of heavy drinking and besides that, it will make you feel good.

If you don't have any good dancing cds, buy as many as you can afford. There is a reason for this. A couple of hours before you leave, play your favorite cds, or if you have a favorite radio station, turn that on. The purpose of this is to get you in the mood for dancing and the nightclub scene.

If you drink, while you are relaxing and listening to the music, drink some of your favorite wine or mixed drinks. Also, taking a hot bath is very relaxing. It's a lot cheaper to drink at home than it is at the clubs. So try to do most of your drinking at home if you want to save some money.

While you are relaxing, picture in your mind's eye, meeting some hot and sexy man at the nightclub. Actually see yourself talking to him, dancing with him, feeling your body rub against him during a slow song, etc. Feel his body next to yours, feel his crotch grinding against yours. See yourself leaving the nightclub and taking him to your place or going to his place or just leaving to get a bite to eat.

You are probably wondering what's the purpose of creating all these images in your mind. These images will register in your subconscious mind and when you get to the nightclub your subconscious mind will give directions to your conscious mind to act them out. Don't be disappointed if this does not work the first time because it takes repetition for this to soak into your subconscious mind. Also, all day long on the day you're going out, keep telling yourself over and over, "I'm going to meet a special man tonight." You will be amazed at the results. This will also help you develop a positive mental attitude and build up your self-confidence.

About thirty minutes before you leave, practice dancing in front of the mirror and looking as sexy as you can. Develop that "I'm crazy about you look" in your eyes. Also, practice smiling in front of the mirror. I'm talking about a nice warm friendly smile, not a phony smile showing all of your teeth.

If you have a cute and sexy smile, use it on men. If you don't have a nice smile, you had better invent one. A good smile can literally melt a man. This makes them feel really special and appreciated. So, practice that sexy smile of yours because it's going to do wonders for you when you approach or be approached by those men in nightclubs. Before you know it, you will be meeting men with just your sexy smile alone.

When approaching a man, always turn on that smile of yours. If you approach him with a real serious and nervous look on your face, you just might scare him. Just a warm, friendly, and relaxed smile will do wonders.

Nightclub "Hot Spots"

As a general rule, it is best to arrive early at a nightclub so you can check out the action. If you arrive late, sometimes the men that you might be attracted to may be already taken up by another woman. Of course there are some nightclubs that do not get going until after midnight. Most men start coming in from 9-11 PM, as a general rule. The men who are shift workers start coming in after 11PM. ideally; the best time to arrive is around 9PM. This way you can see what comes through the door and size up your prospects for the night.

Don't worry about getting a table in the beginning because you are going to be on your feet making the rounds. However, if there is a male prospect sitting at the bar, by all means go and sit beside him and strike up a conversation.

When the action starts picking up, there's going to be favorable places to be standing while approaching the men.

Some women like to stand around by the door and approach a man as he comes in. This does not work too well because of the following reasons:

1. When they first walk in they want to go to the restroom. After all, when nature calls you tend to be in a hurry and don't care to stop and talk to a stranger.
2. They want to go to the restroom to make sure that they look their best.
3. They want to go to the restroom to take drugs.
4. They want to cruise around the nightclub to see if any of their friends are there.
5. They want to walk around to check out the available women.
6. They want to go straight to the bar first to buy a drink.

So you see, it's really not a good idea to stand around and approach them as they walk in. You can go ahead and try it but you will have a lot more success in other areas of the club which I am about to describe.

One of the best places to stand is by the dance floor, especially if you dance. It's even better if the path to the men's restroom goes right by the dance floor. There are men who purposely stand around the dance floor to get asked to dance. This makes it quite easy to ask them to dance or make contact from there. Also, some men like to get a table near the dance floor so they can be asked to dance. I consider the area around the dance floor the best place to make contact.

Another area that is excellent is around the entrance to the mens restroom. Every man will go to the restroom at least once and many times if he's drinking a lot. It's usually not a good idea to approach them before they go into the restroom because they are usually in a hurry to relieve themselves. There is a way around this though, by simply saying, "Can I talk to you when you come out of the restroom?" Normally it is better to approach them when they are coming out of the restroom.

Flirting

While you are cruising the nightclub, keep your flirting eyes out for the man that is alone. He is usually the easiest to meet and attract. He is there for a reason and you can be the lucky woman to fulfill that reason.

Also while walking, keep that sexy-looking gleam in your eye. Literally try to melt men with your eyes. If you make eye contact with a man, make sure you give him a friendly smile and if he is close enough to you, simply say, "Hi." That is all it takes and with practice it will come easy.

If you make eye contact with some man across the way from you and he turns away, don't give up on him. Try to make eye contact again and smile at him. If he smiles back, approach him immediately! This is an opportunity that must not be passed up because it's an open invitation for you to come over and introduce yourself or ask him to dance.

Whatever you do, don't stare at a man. This is impolite and nobody likes to be stared at. Just look at him long enough to make it quite clear that you see him and then immediately look away. What you are saying with your eyes when you look at him this way is, "I know you are there and I would not dream of invading your privacy. Just keep looking at him off and on until you establish some meaningful eye contact and exchange smiles.

So, there you have it, the art of flirting. What really amazes me is these women at the nightclubs that don't even flirt with men. They just stare into space or look down at the floor. If they do accidentally catch the eye of a man, they look away as quickly as possible and let it go at that. They just don't know what they are missing and what they are missing out on is meeting men the easy way.

So my friend, if you're like this, make it a point to stop staring into space and start flirting with men. Flirt with every man in sight. It's a lot of fun and you will be attracting more men than ever before.

How to Approach a Man

Quite simply, all it takes to meet a man in a nightclub is to just walk up to him and start talking to him or by asking him to dance. There's a lot of women who just stand around all night too scared to approach a man or they think they will be approached themselves. Believe me, I know from experience that sometimes you will rarely meet any men just standing around waiting for them to make the first move. You have to make the first move and it comes quite easy after you practice at it. Enough about shy women at clubs. I'm devoting two chapters on shyness and how to overcome this problem.

You're probably wondering "What do I say when I approach a man?" Here are just a few simple opening lines which work well. Feel free to make up your own.

1. "Hi! My name is_____."
2. "Why are you flirting with me?"
3. "What's your name?"
4. "Are you having a good time?"
5. "What's that cologne you're wearing?"
6. "I love your hair. Where do you have it cut?"
7. "Would you like to dance?"
8. "Are you a model?" (Quite a compliment to men)
9. "What kind of drink is that?"
10. This one really works well. Try it and see for yourself. "Excuse me for being so forward, but I couldn't not help but admire the way you danced. Where did you learn to dance like that?" This lays the foundation for starting a conversation. Then you can ask him, "What do you think of this place?" and so on. Then you can ask him to dance.

Many women feel very uncomfortable when approaching men. You're going to have to resolve here and now to put away all your shy ways, fear of rejection, and the other restrictive barriers that keep you from meeting men that you are attracted to. You must assume responsibility for making social contact with men. No matter what technique you use to approach men and no matter how often you use these techniques, you're going to feel a certain amount of discomfort. This is only natural. You must bear the responsibility for meeting others, despite this discomfort.

If you have difficulty approaching men, try this exercise. Force yourself to meet and approach ten men each time you go to a nightclub. Your goal doesn't have to be ten men. You can make it any number you desire. Make it a realistic number though. The main thing is setting that goal. This gives you something to work for and something to accomplish. Look upon this exercise as just practice. Practice for building your social skills for meeting men. Gradually your difficulty in approaching men will disappear. Try this exercise. It really works!

One point you must remember. Most men like to be approached at nightclubs. That's what they are there for. To meet a woman like yourself.

Fast-Dancing

If you don't dance, you'd better learn because a lot of men go to nightclubs to dance and have a good time. You don't have to invest a lot of money in private dancing lessons either. Many cities offer inexpensive dance classes with groups, or perhaps you have a female friend who will teach you.

You don't have to learn fancy dance steps. Just basic free-style dance steps will be sufficient. Besides, in a lot of nightclubs the dance floor is so crowded, there's just not enough room to do any of the sophisticated dance steps, especially on the weekend.

Just simply walk up next to him and say with a smile, "Would you like to dance?" If he says, "No," just say, "OK." You might also say, "Thanks anyway" or even better, "Could I join you for some conversation instead?" Don't stand there and aggravate him by arguing with him as to why he won't dance with you. Just go on to the next man and so on until you find someone to dance with.

Also, look for a man tapping his feet or moving his body to the beat of the music. This usually means that he is anxious to dance. If he's dancing with himself while standing, this also means that he's dying to dance.

Don't forget to dance to the slow songs, even though they don't play too many at most nightclubs. Don't pass up these good opportunities to get instant physical contact with men.

So now you're out on the dance floor dancing to a fast song. While you're dancing with him, make eye contact. Just catch his eye and hold it momentarily, then look away. Repeat this process until you start getting a smile out of him or at least a look of interest. Of course, now some men won't look at you while you are dancing. They don't focus their eyes on anyone in particular and just look at their feet, the floor, or they're busy trying to show off in front of everyone else. Some men are self-conscious about everybody watching them, so they don't make much eye contact. Anyway, try to establish as much eye contact as possible. This will be to your advantage.

While you're dancing this first dance together, be sure and make some verbal contact no matter how loud the music is. The first thing you should say is, "What's your name?" After he tells you his name, tell him yours. Now you have become formally introduced, just by dancing. Also, make a comment on how nice he looks or compliment his clothes, jewelry, smile, etc.

So now this first song is coming to an end. When it ends don't hesitate and look at him to see if he wants to dance to the next record. Just turn away from him while continuing to dance and look at him out of the corner of your eye to see what he is going to do. You see, by hesitating at the end of a song, you force a direct confrontation on whether to dance to the next song. If you just keep on dancing into the next song, taking it for granted that he wants to dance again; you'll be more successful in keeping him out on the dance floor. The longer you dance with him the better your chances of getting to know him.

Now we get to the part when you finish dancing. This will usually end in these following ways:

1. He stops dancing and says, "Thank you."
2. You're both hot, sweaty, and exhausted from dancing and mutually agree to leave the dance floor.
3. Either one of you develops a cramp and has to leave the dance floor. Has this ever happened to you?

This is very important! After you have finished dancing whatever you do, don't let him get away after thanking you for the dance. Just simply say, "Can I join you for a drink?" Also, you could say, "Can I talk to you about something?" After this statement, he will say, "Talk about what?" Then you say, "I'll tell you when you when we sit down." After this, just start making conversation. Also, if he doesn't have a table and he is just standing like yourself, just say, "Can I talk to you for a little while?"

So, what you do after you finish dancing can determine the future of your whole night and whether you're going to become intimate with a man or not. What I can't figure out are these women that dance with a man and don't even look at or talk to him while they are dancing and when they finish, she says, "Thanks" and just walks away. Needless to say, you don't meet any men this way.

So when you have finished dancing, move right in for the kill. Don't hesitate; just proceed immediately with determination that you're going to make contact with this man.

Slow-Dancing

Let me give you a few pointers if you're slow-dancing and by all means try to dance to every slow dance because of the physical contact involved.

Just as in fast dancing, immediately start introduction procedures. Open up by saying, "My name is_____ What's yours?

When slow-dancing, try to hold him as close to your body as possible. Gently now! Don't squeeze him like an octopus. When moving your right leg, gently brush his inner thighs. While dancing, gently squeeze his hand and see if you get any response. If you do, continue with the next step. Start rubbing his back with your hand. At this point if he starts rubbing your shoulders, neck, or back and starts grinding his crotch against yours, you are on your way. At this stage of the game it's time to try and kiss him. Begin kissing him on the neck and work your way up to behind the ear, then the ear lobe, then kiss him on the lips. If you've gotten this far, chances are you're going to become intimate with him tonight, if not later for sure. If you have tried all these moves and you do not get any response, don't be concerned about it. Some men are reluctant to show any affection towards a total stranger. This is quite common, so don't jump to conclusions thinking that he's cold or not interested in you.

Chapter 2 - Where to Meet Men

The following recommendations on where to meet men is one of the most extensive information on this subject ever published:

The Hitchhiker WARNING: Use this information at your own risk

How many times have you seen a guy thumbing for a ride? At least once and probably a few times.

Like most women, you probably just passed these guys and kept right on going. Well my friend, you may have just passed up a potential golden opportunity.

So the next time you see a male hitchhiker, by all means, think about picking him up. If he's going the opposite direction, make a U-turn and go back and pick him up.

I know what you're thinking already. It's too dangerous to pick up men thumbing for a ride. The majority of male hitchhikers are not dangerous. I'll leave it up to you if you want to take advantage of this opportunity to meet men.

You are probably wondering now what to do after you have picked him up. The first thing to do is ask him where he's going. This will give you an idea of how far he intends to ride with you and you'll know how much time you'll have to make your approach to get to know him better.

If you follow my conversational guidelines outlined in my chapter on how to talk to a man, you'll establish a warm rapport. After you've established some friendly contact, just ask him, "I'd like to see you again. Would you mind if I give you a call sometime?" Hopefully he will give you his phone number and you can follow up on him later. If you're traveling out of town and pick up a man on the highway, ask him if he'd like to stop and get something to eat so you can talk and get to know him better.

Parties

Never, never turn down a party invitation. Whether it be friends, a beach party, office party, etc. Parties are a real gold mine for meeting men. The atmosphere is very sociable and conducive for flirtations.

All you've got to do is walk up to a man you're interested in and introduce yourself. Then follow up with your conversational skills.

Also, it's a good idea to throw your own party. Invite everyone you can think of. For instance, if it's a male friend you invite, ask him to invite some of his male friends. If it's a female friend, ask her to invite some of her male friends. This way your party will be stocked with an ample supply of men. This will give you an opportunity to meet some new men and make friends.

When at a party, whatever you do, don't stand in a corner. Be sure to mingle and flirt with as many men as possible. There's nothing to fear because people will be friendly and rejections are rare unless you make a fool of yourself.

Daytime Barfly's

These are men who hang out at bars during the day. They are bored and friendly. They are also very easy to meet.

So if you're off during the day, check out your local bars during the day. If you see a man alone in the bar, approach him immediately and ask him, "Can I join you for some conversation?"

Volunteer Activities

There are numerous organizations looking for voluntary workers. By doing volunteer work, you will most likely be exposed to some nice men and you will be working together for a common cause. You just can't help but get to know men well when you're working together. This leaves the door wide open for forming intimate relationships.

There are plenty of activities that you can volunteer for. Examples are: Charity work, political campaigns, hospital work, crisis hot-line counselors, church functions, working with retarded and underprivileged children, telethons, carnivals, bazaars, teaching courses, party host, and many, many more.

How do you find volunteer work? Just check your newspapers. Here in Houston there's a special section in the newspaper listing organizations looking for volunteers, giving details and how to contact them. Keep your eyes and ears open for volunteer opportunities.

Volunteer for anything. Even if it's your job. Volunteer for special functions such as company picnics, dinners, banquets, planning company trips, recreation committee, etc. This will pay off in contacts with all those lovely men at work.

Hotels and Motels

I realize it could be expensive to just rent a room for a day, in hope of meeting men. However, it could pay off in big dividends. What you can do to cut down on expenses is to share the room with a couple of your female friends and all three of you go man-hunting. Hotels and motels are great places to approach the world's easiest target for a casual affair (the man on a business trip or vacation). He's more relaxed and casual and he's away from the prying eyes of family, friends, and neighbors. He will let his hair down and he doesn't have to worry about his reputation or what people think, being that he's away from home.

The best places to approach men are at the pool, club, or restaurant.

In conclusion, I might add that if you don't want to rent a room, you can still meet men at hotels and motels. The clubs are open to the public, so it's fair game in there and it's a good place to hang out and meet out-of-towners. Also, you can drive to a hotel or motel in your bathing suit and hang around the pool and strike up a conversation with all those men. Be sure and bring a change of clothes with you in case you want to go somewhere afterwards.

Parks

This is a great place to meet men. Some men go by themselves to meditate and think about their problems. Some go to read and even some go just to meet women.

If you see a man all alone looking sad and blue, approach him and say, "You look sad; can I be of any help?" He just may pour his heart out to you.

If you see a man walking a dog, approach him and say, "That sure is a cute dog you have there. What's his name?" This can open the door for more conversation.

You might want to bring your frisbee with you and ask a man, "Do you want to toss some frisbee?"

What you can do when you go to a park is bring a picnic blanket, a bottle of wine, and lunch for two. When you spot a man you like, set up your blanket and picnic supplies near him. Then just invite him to join you. You can really have some fun times this way.

The Supermarket

This is an overlooked place to meet men. These places are just crawling with men. With a little confidence, this is an excellent place to approach men. Here's some examples of approaches to use: Hang around the meat section and when you see a man you'd like to meet, approach him and ask him, "How long do you broil chicken?" Then you can follow up with, "Gee, I wish I knew how to cook. How did you learn to cook? Did your mother teach you?" The main objective is to get a conversation going and see if he'd like to get together sometime. Another good place for the approach is in the produce department. Just pick out the vegetable of your choice and ask him how to cook it.

Tennis

Take a look around at the tennis courts. What will you see? Plenty of men. That's what. Tennis is very popular and attracts a lot of men. Lots of men may go to the tennis courts to meet women. Perhaps not openly, but subconsciously.

Tennis is a one-on-one sport and this allows for a lot of mental concentration between you. It sure is a good way of getting to know someone. Just the two of you having fun together. What's good too is that after you have played a match, it's quite natural to cool off and talk to each other and perhaps go and have a drink or get a bite to eat.

How do you approach men at the tennis courts? There are a lot of different approaches. You can say, "Do you need a partner?" Or you could reserve a court in advance and say to a man, "Would you like to play on Court 9? My tennis partner didn't show up."

You might want to arrive early to shoot the bull before you play tennis. Just talk to any and every man you see. This way you can meet men before you even make it to the courts.

If you don't play tennis, by all means take lessons. This opens up another avenue for meeting men. Let me say that you don't have to become an expert. Basic skills will get you by because most of the guys you'll be playing later won't be that good either.

I would suggest playing at public tennis courts. You'll see more of a variety of different men there. Tennis clubs are very expensive and you'll see the same old faces a lot.

A word about tennis attire. It would be worth it to invest in some nice pro-type tennis wear. It will make you look like a tennis pro and these outfits really turn some men on.

In conclusion, I want to tell you about a device to use to attract men and make you popular. When you play tennis, always bring a large jug filled with lemonade, kool-aid, or Gator-Aide. Also, you can even bring a small ice chest filled with cokes. All you have to do is ask a man on the court "Would you like something cold to drink?" After you've worked up a sweat or if it's a hot day, something cold to drink really hits the spot and is hard to turn down.

Jogging

Jogging is a fantastic way to meet men and besides that, it's good for your health, mind and body.

Pick out a jogging area and start running on a regular basis. By observation, you will notice men that arrive each day at the same place and around the same time. Jogging trails and parks are wonderful for unhurried seduction, because you're going to see him again and again, so you can work on him a little at a time.

During the week the men are usually out between 6 and 8 AM, around noon, and between 5 and 8 PM. Weekends are usually best because you will see them jogging throughout the day.

Let me explain the approach to use on jogging trails that will work well for you. Always jog with a towel around your neck and wear a small plastic bottle filled with lemonade, Gator-Aid, or water around your neck. Then you will jog beside a man and offer him a drink and your towel to wipe the sweat off of his face. Then you invite him to sit down and take a breather so you can talk.

Roller Rinks

This is a hot activity that has swept the nation. The roller discos are particularly popular. They have light shows and a good sound system.

It may have never occurred to you that this is a hot spot for meeting men. Believe me; these places are abundant with men. A lot of them go to the rinks to have fun and meet women.

You might be saying to yourself, "I'd like to go but I don't know how to skate." Well don't let that hold you back. Skating is very easy and you will be able to pick it up rather quickly without lessons. Of course, with practice, you'll get a lot better. If you don't have skates, that's no problem. You can rent them.

If you're a good skater and you see a man having problems, offer to help him learn how to skate. He surely will appreciate it and this is another good way to meet guys at the skating rink.

Art Galleries

Go to any art gallery (especially on the weekends) and you'll see plenty of men. Some of these men aren't just there because of their appreciation for art. They may be there to meet a woman like yourself.

An art gallery provides a perfect setting to approach men. The atmosphere is very friendly and the men aren't going to feel uptight and threatened when you try to meet them.

Approaching a man in an art gallery is very simple. All you have to do is walk over to a man standing in front of a painting and make a comment on the painting. Another variation to this is to stand in front of a painting yourself and when a man passes by, you make a comment to him about the painting. After you've made contact say, "Would you mind if I tour the gallery with you?" Afterwards you can invite him out to get something to eat or to go have a drink somewhere.

Skiing

Skiing resorts are real "hot" meeting spots consisting of mostly singles and groups. You won't see many couples and you will see plenty of men. I'd highly recommend spending part of your annual vacation at a ski resort.

How do I plan a skiing vacation? Just contact your local travel agent and they will be able to assist you. Some airlines offer ski tour packages and charter flights. These charter flights are golden opportunities because all of you will be going to the same destination. You'll be able to make friends on the plane. Be sure and sit next to a man or a group of men. Then just strike up a conversation. This way you can have some men lined up before you even get to the resort.

You may be saying to yourself, "I don't know how to ski." Well this is no problem. There will be a lot of beginners there just like yourself. You'll need to take lessons and there are a lot of advantages to this. You'll be exposed to lots of men in the class and will have opportunities to meet them. Just be sure and take group lessons so you'll be exposed to a number of men.

You can meet men first at the ski lift. Everyone will be standing around chatting while waiting to go up the lift. Being that most lifts have chairs built for two people, just ask a man, "Would you like to ride up with me? Most rides are of a long duration, so you'll have plenty of time to converse on the way up.

Nightlife is booming and the action is hot around the resorts. The bars, nightclubs, and restaurants are loaded with nice men looking for a good time. That's where you come in at.

So what are you waiting for? Why not plan a ski trip and have the time of your life?

Department Stores

These are great places for meeting men and salesmen and are literally just crawling with lots of young attractive men.

Meeting salesmen is very easy. They are usually fairly attractive and are usually bored and would welcome a woman like yourself approaching them and brightening up their day. All you have to do is simply pretend you are shopping for a gift for your father or brother and ask him for assistance. After you have spent some time with him talking and making contact, suggest meeting for a cup of coffee or a drink on his lunch break or after he gets off.

As for the shoppers in the stores, let me offer some approaches:

When you see a man loaded down with purchases, offer to help him carry his packages. This has drawbacks though because he might not trust a stranger carrying his packages. He may fear that you'll run off with them. It's worth a try though. All he can do is say no and think of the possibilities if he says yes.

Another approach is to walk up to a man pretending you need help with a purchase. For example, if you're in a jewelry store, approach a man and say, "I'm shopping for a watch for my brother and I was wondering if you would try this watch on so I can see how it looks?" 99 out of 100 times he will help you. After that, just turn on your charm and conversational skills and ask him out.

A good place to approach men is at the cologne counters. He will tend to take his time in this department. Your approach? Look for a man trying on some cologne and get next to him and give him your opinion of that exotic scent he just tried on.

Restaurants

This is an overlooked great place to meet men. Using some special techniques, you can be successful in meeting men here. Here are the techniques:

1. If you see a man across the way you'd like to meet, just simply use the waiter or waitress as a messenger. Now, instruct him to bring this man a drink and a note saying, "Hi! My name is Susan from across the way in the blue blouse and curly blond hair and I'm irresistibly attracted to you and I'd love to meet you. Will you come over and join me?"

2. If you see a man you'd like to meet at a counter or table with an empty chair, just make it a point to sit next to him. Then you ask him, "Excuse me, I've never eaten here before and I was wondering if you could recommend something good to eat?" This breaks the ice and then you follow up with your conversational skills.

3. As a variation to technique number one, ask your waiter or waitress to ask if he'd mind if the woman in the blue blouse and curly blond hair across the way joined him.

Transportation

If you commute by train, bus, plane, subways, etc., there's going to be golden opportunities to meet men. These places are filled with eligible, attractive men.

The whole trick to meeting them is to make it a point to take a seat next to them. This way you've got him pinned in and he's not going anywhere unless you scare him off. If you're on a train or plane, he doesn't have much choice.

All you've got to do when sitting next to him is to just start talking to him. Talk to him about anything and turn on that charm of yours.

If you take a bus or train to work or school, pick out any male riders you'd like to meet. Select one and make it a point to sit near or close to him. Do this each time you see him and after seeing you a few times you'll practically be old friends, even if you haven't spoken to each other.

Churches

You'll always find plenty of single, nice men at church.

Many churches have begun to sponsor activities for singles. These activities range from dances and trips to lectures and discussions, from seminars on communication to workshops on sexuality.

If the church doesn't have a singles group, you'll have to use the conventional approach. Pick out a church and start going there regularly. Each time you go make it a point to sit next to or near the men of your choice.

Try to be near this man each time you go to church. You'll become old friends before too long. The first chance you get, ask him if you could talk to him after the service. He will probably say yes and you'll be on your way.

Human Potential Groups

These groups function to lay all the ground work to help people lead a happier and fulfilled life. Examples of such groups are Silva Mind Control, Actualizations, EST, Transactional Analysis, Dale Carnegie courses, etc. A majority of these groups follow the pioneering work of Abraham Maslow and Carl Rogers in humanistic psychology, the therapy groups of the 1960's, and the eclectic Esalen Institute total experience.

These groups provide an excellent vehicle for one to meet other singles. A large number of people attending these training sessions are unmarried.

Human potential group workshops provide a relaxed atmosphere to meet others. You don't feel pressured to meet others like you would if you were in a singles bar. You're both there for a common cause and this brings people together. The people there are eager to meet others and the men are friendly. These groups create conditions under which friendships and relationships can flourish.

So, why not look into joining one of these groups? It can bring beneficial change into your life and give you new insights, not to mention meeting lots of new men and establishing new friendships.

Health Clubs

This is the best of both worlds. You can get your body into shape while at the same time, shape up your love-life.

They offer activities such as racquetball, swimming, tennis, whirlpools, saunas, and exercise. These offer excellent opportunities for meeting men. All you have to do is ask him to join you in a game of racquetball or even challenge him to a race across the pool. The saunas and whirlpools are hot spots too. Just imagine yourself relaxing in a whirlpool filled with hot and sexy men. Think of the possibilities!

A final word in selecting a health club. Be sure to shop around and check out their facilities. A majority of the clubs will give you a free trial day. This way you can check out the men in these clubs and what kind of setup there is for meeting them.

In conclusion, I'd like to mention, you'd be surprised how many men join these clubs just to meet women. Keep this in mind when you become a member, even though it is going to be a little expensive. Believe me; you'll get your money's worth!

Swimming Pools

This is one of the greatest places to meet men. I'm going to be talking mainly about apartment swimming pools.

Here are the techniques I used successfully to meet men at the pool:

You're going to need some very important equipment. Your appearance is very important and you want to make a good impression upon entering the pool area. I would suggest wearing a stylish bathing suit. Cosmopolitan magazine offers some good examples and your local department stores.

Also, I'd suggest wearing some nice thongs, sun glasses, an unusual hat, and a Hawaiian or surfer shirt. The idea is to create that refined look and not to look like a bum.

Your most important item to bring with you is your ice chest. Stock it with an assortment of liquor. I'd suggest some beer, wine, coke, and pre-made mixed drinks that come in cans you can purchase at your local liquor store. Don't forget the plastic bar glasses! Also bring your inflatable air mattress and an extra one if possible, and a good-sounding radio.

OK, now you're looking the part and you've got all your attraction ammunition with you. Let's take it step by step using these proven techniques:

You've entered the pool area. Make a complete circle around the pool to check out the available men. While you're walking and you catch the eye of a male, instantly remark, "Hi" or "Hello" or "It sure is a pretty day isn't it?" If you get a response, keep walking and make a circle and come back to him. When you return, ask him, "Can I join you?" Most likely he won't mind. Introduce yourself and offer him a drink. Turn on your radio and ask him if there's any particular station he would like to listen to. To establish some physical contact, ask him to rub some sun tan oil on your back. If you've played your cards right and turned on your charm and conversational skills, you should be on your way.

Another technique to use is what I call the old "air mattress technique." Here is how it works: Sit your ice chest on the edge of the pool to where you have access to it while laying on your air mattress. Now, get on your air mattress with a can of beer or mixed drink in hand (I might add that it would be a good idea to try and keep your hair dry. This way you'll look more attractive. A person with wet hair is not very eye-appealing). Maneuver your air mattress around the pool and park it across from a male near the pool. Then just simply remark, "You sure are getting a nice tan today." This breaks the ice and then follow up with, "I've got an extra air mattress. Would you like to join me?" This technique will really work for you successfully and I highly recommend that you try it. Also, if there are other males in the pool on air mattresses pull up beside them and feed them the same opening lines.

Tours

This is an excellent way to meet male tourists and these tours have some lonely attractive males.

Every major city has walking or bus tours. Cities on the water usually have boat tours of some type. Check the yellow pages under "tours" or google tours in your city to find out information on the tours. Sign up for one of the tours on the weekend.

Meeting these men on a tour is easy as pie. All you've got to do for openers is to make a comment on what the tour guide is showing you. Also, it would really be a good idea to bring a digital camera along with you so you can take a picture of him to take back home with him.

After the tour is completed, ask him if you can take him on a personal guided tour of some unique places in the city. Being that you live there, I'm sure you can think of some great places to take him.

So why not try this method of meeting men. It's a uniquely different way of meeting men and some of the tours are very interesting. The atmosphere is great and the people are relaxed and friendly.

Theater Groups

Large metropolitan areas have numerous amateur theater groups. They can also be found in small communities. These groups are full of nice men. Backstage romances are very common.

Contact one of these groups and volunteer your services. If you act or feel like you could act, try and land a part. If possible, try to select a part where you will kiss or hug an actor. A professional actor wouldn't take these things to heart but a small town guy will get off on them. Your reward, of course, comes when he accepts an invitation to your home to "rehearse."

If you don't care to act, there are plenty of activities you can participate in such as prop, stagehand, set designer, advertising, ticket taker, etc. Take anything, even if it's cleanup. The main objective is participation.

You'll be working with the crew and will be spending a lot of time together. You'll become close and you will feel like one big family. This leaves the door open to intimate relationships with the opposite sex.

Another advantage to working with a theater group is that you will be participating in a lot of social activities. There will be backstage get-togethers and lots of parties. These are golden opportunities for meeting the men.

Look into this way of meeting men. It will be a lot of fun and increase your circle of friends.

Friends, Relatives, and Co-workers

This is an ideal way to meet men. Just make a list of all your friends, relatives, and co-workers. Then contact them by phone or in person and ask them if they know of any single men they could introduce you to. It's nothing to be embarrassed about when asking. You're just wanting some male companionship.

Meeting men this way is very natural and these people can usually tell you a lot about the man. Some will really enjoy playing the role of cupid. Who knows, you may meet the love of your life, just by asking around.

In conclusion, here's the script to use when contacting these people: "I am expanding my social circle of male friends. Could you introduce me to some of your single male friends?"

At Work

Take a real good look around you when you're at work. Depending on how large of a company you work for and what type of work you do, you're going to see a lot of eligible men. Don't pass up these opportunities to meet men. You can make a lot of social contacts, being that you spend a lot of your time at work.

At a very large company you may actually have anywhere from a hundred to a thousand men to choose from. Talk about heaven on earth! Places of employment are hotbeds for romance and behind the scenes activities.

How do you approach men at work? Just introduce yourself. Say, "Hi, my name is _____. I work in the _____ dept. Being that we work for the same company, I thought I'd introduce myself." Then carry on a conversation from there. Don't forget to charm and compliment him.

After you've gotten to know him and established some rapport, ask him out to lunch. Who knows, that could lead to an intimate relationship.

A word about any new men at work. Be sure and hit up on them right away. Don't let the other women beat you to the punch. Welcome him to the company and try to make him feel at home. Introduce him to your co-workers. Invite him to join your lunch group for something to eat.

Finally, don't pass up any company parties, picnics, trips, bowling or softball leagues, banquets, etc. These are great for meeting and mingling with your male co-workers.

The Beach

This is one of the more favorable and popular spots to meet men. They are there for the taking. Take your pick! The beach provides a perfect setting for meeting men. It's a casual and relaxed atmosphere and most of the men are friendly. It's just simply a matter of approaching them and talking to them. That's all there is to it.

A lot of girls make the mistake of going to the beach and just stare at men and they stroll up and down the beach not even smiling or saying, "Hi" to men as they walk along. They don't even stop to talk to a guy that catches their eye. They just don't have the guts to approach them. What's really sad is that these men are there to have a good time and attract the opposite sex. Why do you think they spend all that time at the gym building their muscles? It's to turn you on.

So be bold and you'll be surprised how easy it is to meet men at the beach.

Now, I will describe some important techniques and strategies to use at the beach. Use them and you can't fail and you will have the summer of your life!

It's important how you dress for the beach. Dress well and don't just wear a pair of old cut-offs with holes in them. Wear a nice designer bathing suit. Also, while not sunning, wear a shirt appropriate for the beach such as a tank top or colorful T-shirt.

Invest in some nice attractive sunglasses (not the cheap kind). Try on several different styles and select the one that makes you look unique and different.

Now, you'll be all decked out for the beach and you'll stand out from the rest of the ordinary girls. What this means is that you'll attract the attention of the opposite sex and that's what you're striving for.

You should bring some very important equipment that you'll use in meeting men. These are as follows:

1. ICE CHEST - This is your most important item. Fill it with beer, wine, mixed drinks in a can, and soft drinks. You'll use this to offer a guy a drink when you've approached a man.
2. BLANKET - Bring a blanket big enough for you and a guy to lie on. Make sure it's clean and attractive and not old and smelly.
3. FRISBEE, VOLLEYBALL, BEACH BALL, and FOOTBALL - With these you can approach a guy and ask, "Want to play?"
4. RADIO - This comes in handy. What to do is lay near a guy or group of guys and turn on your radio. Then you ask, "What station would you like to hear?" This opens the door for further conversation.
5. BODY SURFING BOARD - Buy two of them. They are cheap and made of styrofoam. Approach a guy and ask him if he'd like to do some body surfing.
6. SURFBOARD - If you do surf this can be an advantage. Some guys are very attracted to surfers. Some guys don't know how to surf and have never even been on a surfboard. If you surf, all you have to do is approach a guy and ask him, "Would you like to learn how to surf?" If you don't know how to surf yourself you can always fake it. It will be a lot of fun trying anyway.
7. SUN TAN OIL - Here's one that will always work. Approach a guy and ask him, "Would you rub some sun tan oil on my back?" You'll never get turned down and it really feels good having a guy rubbing your back.

While walking the beach looking for guys, when a guy catches your eye, give him a warm smile and say, "Hi." If he responds, don't keep walking whatever you do. Stop immediately and start talking to him. Invite him over to your blanket and offer him something to drink or you can invite him to go in the water. Also you can ask him if he wants to play some beach sports such as frisbee, volleyball, beach ball, etc.

If you pass a guy that you're interested in and he has his eyes closed, just approach him and say, "Weren't you on the cover of GQ Magazine?" He will be flattered and this opens up a conversation.

In conclusion, I hope I've given you some new ideas you have never thought of before on how to meet guys at the beach. Happy hunting!

Adult Education Classes and University Extension Courses

Most good-sized communities in the United States offer adult education courses. The courses are varied and offer something for everyone. The classes are held at convenient times for full time workers and are available at no cost or for a small fee.

These courses are an excellent channel for meeting men.

The key to it all is to take courses that appeal to men. Let me offer some suggestions of courses that will be made up of mostly men: Sports, investing, auto repair, writing, computer repair, etc. By taking these courses you will be one of the few women in the class. You will be surrounded by men and you will get all the attention and you will be in demand. The men will be literally fighting amongst themselves for your attention.

Let me tell you about my friend Sandra who took an auto repair class at my urging. This is what she told me about the class: "Well, there were fifteen men in the class and I was the only woman. Most of them were single and most of them were around my age. Now, I've only been to three of the classes and have three more to go and I've already dated three of the men...and I'm becoming a great mechanic on top of it. You know Sandra; this was a really great idea of yours. Probably none of these men would have talked to me if I had approached them in a supermarket or on the street, but no man refuses to talk to you over pasta."

A word of advice. Arrive at the classes early. Everyone sits around and shoots the bull and the atmosphere is very relaxed and there's no pressure to meet someone like in a singles bar. By arriving early you can make the rounds and converse with the men before class.

Male Strip Joints

I sincerely hope you're not one of those women who go to strip joints just to watch the exotic male dancers. Most women do and they don't know what they are missing out on. These men can be picked up and are generally easy to meet. A lot of women don't even try to pick them up and it's a shame because these guys need lovin just like any other man.

How do you approach these men? Well, normally they will be approaching you, possibly to hustle you for drinks or a table dance. Don't hold this against them and think they're just trying to take you for a ride. They're just trying to make a living and they may get a commission on these drinks.

You might as well face the facts that you just might have to buy them a drink or table dance to talk to them. These can be house rules.

Buy them a drink or two, it won't kill you. Just be nice to them and treat them with respect and you can get somewhere with them.

OK, let's say you've bought a male dancer a drink and he's sitting with you (possibly on your lap, kissing you). Turn on your charm and conversational skills at this point. Ask him if he'd like to go out for breakfast when he gets off. This will usually be after hours. If he declines, don't let this discourage you. He may have other plans or may just not feel like it. Then ask him if he'd like to go out to dinner on his day off. And by all means you need to ask him if you could give him a call sometimes. You'd really be surprised how easy they are to date and they are very friendly.

You're going to run into the type that is very wild and promiscuous. They will go to bed with anyone. Also, you may run into male dancers that are prostitutes on the side. And of course, some will be supporting a drug habit. You will meet all kinds and most of them are guys that you would enjoy dating and have a good time with.

Make it a point to pick out a strip joint and go there regularly at the same time and the same day of the week. You will usually see the same dancers. You'll become a familiar face and become friends with all the dancers. There's a lot of competition sometimes among the dancers for the girlfriends of the other dancers. They will actually try to steal each other's girlfriends away from each other. Wouldn't you like to have a bunch of hot exotic dancers fighting over you? Talk about heaven!

A word about spending money. Don't throw it around trying to impress the men, especially if you can't afford it. They are used to this and it doesn't impress them that much. When they keep pressuring you for drinks and you want to stop buying them drinks, just explain to him that you know the ropes of this business and you'd rather spend your money on him away from the club. He will understand.

In conclusion, don't sit around and drool and stare at these men anymore. Make an effort to meet and attract these men. Don't beat around the bush with them. Just come right out and tell him that you want to see him when he's off work.

Chapter 3 - Internet Dating Services

Do you need an internet dating service? It is important to decide first if you really need to join a dating service. I received and read many comments from people who reported having had much better success with other methods of meeting qualified potential mates than with dating services. Many mentioned personal ads in local and national newspapers and magazines have been more successful for them. Others mentioned such things as joining local single's clubs, volunteer organizations, church sponsored groups, etc. Still others suggest asking your friends or family to introduce you to someone. Since internet dating services can be expensive, you may wish to try these and other methods in this book to meet men.

If after you try, or you have already tried, these suggestions, and nothing else has worked, then maybe an internet dating service should be considered. You can not be too careful in selecting and dealing with these services. Please read and understand this chapter before you start your search for a service.

Computer Dating Services - You Do The Choosing

People used to be reluctant to admit that they used computer dating services, there was a certain stigma attached to the whole process. Not anymore. Today more and more busy people are finding that using the internet to help them find love is just a smart thing to do.

It's not just that we are too busy to find love on our own, we just are more comfortable with doing all kinds of things online. We know that the old methods of meeting someone special were hit and miss at best.

With all the online social networks and places to connect with people that share your interests, it just makes sense to put that same technology to use for finding someone to date, or possibly even marry.

There are a lot of computer dating services online, and some are better than others. They are also not all focused on the same thing. Some are purely focused on helping those that are looking for a serious relationship. Others are focused on helping those that are only looking for something casual.

Whatever you are looking for: serious, casual, or even just a friend, there are sites online that will help you find that special someone.

Many sites will even allow you to sign up for free and look around a little bit. If you are interested in meeting someone close to you, this is a great way to go. You can see how many people there are in your area before you actually pay to join.

These sites will require you to upgrade to a paid membership to utilize all the features of the site. In many cases you can look but you can't communicate with anyone else on the site until you upgrade to a paid membership.

Also, some sites pride themselves on their 'scientific' matching techniques while others allow you to pick and choose and talk to anyone who you think looks interesting and find out for yourself if the two of you have a connection.

It's up to you to decide which method makes you the most comfortable. Another very important aspect of your online dating is to fill out an interesting profile. This is the first 'meeting' someone will have with you. The more you let them know about the type of person you are and what you are looking for, the better chance you'll have of connecting with someone with similar interests.

One word of caution though, while you want to give a complete profile that doesn't mean that you have to include such personal information as where you work, your full name or real name and certainly not where you live. Tell them about who you are without letting them know too much.

Meeting someone online can make it really easy to get to know each other. It usually starts as exchanging emails, which takes a lot of the pressure off since you have time to think of what to say and don't have to worry about being tongue tied.

You can also use webcams to chat as you get more comfortable with each other. By the time the two of you actually meet, you should already have a lot of chemistry and even a little bit of history' which is what makes computer dating services so great.

Dating Singles Online

If you are thinking about dating singles online, you are one of many. This is a great way for people who are busy or can't get out to meet singles for other reasons to interact with others who are looking for a relationship.

Get to Know the Guidelines

If you haven't dated online before, you should get to know some of the tips and guidelines that are generally held. While online dating has similarities to dating in person, there are also some big differences. Not only should you have an idea of online dating etiquette so you don't offend someone, you should also be able to tell when you should or shouldn't be offended by someone else's behavior.

A good example of this when you are dating singles online is that it is not only acceptable to talk to many different potential dates at once, but it is encouraged. The whole point of being online is to meet a bunch of people and talk to them. Don't be afraid to be in contact with a bunch of people.

But generally once you have begun actually dating someone, you need to put your account on hold. You don't have to do this on your first or second date, but once you decide to pursue a relationship with someone, freeze your account out of respect for them and others who don't want to date someone who may already be involved.

Understand What is Good to Say and What is Not

When you are dating singles online, you need to learn about how to talk to them. One major issue is using abbreviations. People have been shown to have a poor response to messages that exchange u for you, or ur for your or you're. Any shortening of words like this isn't attractive, and neither is leaving out capitalization or punctuation such as apostrophes.

Think about it, when you are communicating with someone online, they have very little to go on when it comes to figuring out who you are. Your picture and profile give them some idea, but it is your words and how you use them that really show your colors to other people.

Also, when you are dating singles online, don't use terms that sound like pick-up lines. Women in particular should avoid referring to a man as hot or sexy. While the guy might think this is a compliment, if used too early a man might think the woman is only after one thing, and this usually turns men off.

Be Honest!

There are few pieces of advice more important than this. Trying to be someone you aren't can take many forms, such as having an old picture up, leaving things off your profile that are a big part of who you are, or putting things on your profile that aren't true.

More people complain of dishonesty in online dating than anything else.

Dating singles online can be very rewarding, and you just may find the perfect someone. By getting acquainted with the guidelines and etiquette you will impress people, and by being true to yourself you will enjoy your experience a lot more.

5 Benefits of Dating Singles Online

If you are looking for companionship, then you are now, or soon to be, counted among the growing number of dating singles online. Dating websites are more popular than ever, and still growing. There are several reasons why this is the case, some of which may surprise you.

1. Trying something new. It doesn't take long for single people to get tired of the traditional dating scene. It's either too boring, time-consuming or otherwise demanding. When dating singles online the problems of traditional dating virtually disappear. Sure, you

still have to sort through several people, but the way the "hunt" is conducted is entirely different.

2. Convenience. You don't have to spend a lot of time getting ready when dating online. All you have to do is log in to the dating website of your choice, look at profiles, and maybe exchange a few messages. This takes much less time than getting dressed up and driving somewhere. If all goes well, you will eventually meet someone face-to-face, but until then, you don't have to worry about the normal inconveniences.

3. A large pool. No, this isn't referring to a nice place to swim. Rather, it refers to the fact that there is a large pool of potential dating partners available online. After all, you are connecting to people from all over (though there are sites that cater to smaller areas). You no longer have to choose from the same dozen or so regulars at your local single's bar. Instead, you may have access to thousands and thousands of profiles.

4. Variety. Maybe you live in a small town and love the works of Voltaire, professional wrestling, scrapbooking and Czech cheeses. It may be nearly impossible to find anyone in your area that shares those interests. With the massive variety of dating online singles, your chances of finding someone with the same tastes goes up significantly. Of course, those with more standard tastes are out there, too.

5. Anonymity. But isn't the whole idea of online dating to get to know someone? It is, but by being anonymous early on, you can feel more at ease being yourself. When somebody isn't looking at your profile, it doesn't feel like they are giving you the cold shoulder. It's not you as a person they aren't responding to, it's the data contained in your profile. Also, if you happen to get rejected, you won't take it as personally because you are not as emotionally invested. Rejection works both ways, though, and online dating takes care of that problem, too. If you aren't interested in somebody, all you need to do is move on to another profile; all without the fear of guilt.

Traditional dating isn't going away, but with all it has going for it, online dating is becoming a more and more serious competitor. Oh, and the best thing of all? The chance to meet somebody special and be happy.

The Do's And Dont's Of Computer Dating

Computer dating can be a great way to meet people who are compatible with your interests. It can allow non-threatening introductions, and let you meet lots of others. Sometimes it develops long term relationships.
While computer dating is very popular and generally safe, you should take some precautions. Dating is, by definition, a personal thing, and you should be cautious about giving out personal information online.

Choosing a reputable service is the first step you'll want to take. Talk to friends about sites they've had good experiences with. See if any of the couples you know met online.

It's also important to check out the reviews of computer dating services. You won't want to make a judgment from one review. But if you keep reading the same complaints over and over, you'll likely want to avoid the site.

One of the great benefits of computer dating is that you can meet people from all over that have the same interests that you have. If you have an unusual hobby, you can specify that in your profile. If you want to meet others of the same faith, you can join sites especially for your faith.

After you choose a site and post a profile, you may have people request a contact. You may see others you'd like to meet. Just take it very slowly at first. Initiate a conversation, but keep your information anonymous.

You should have lots of online conversations before you set up a face-to-face meeting. Be very discriminating about continuing relationships. If there are any red flags, you'll want to proceed very cautiously or end the relationship before meeting. You don't need to invite excess drama into your life, and you want to stay safe.

Set realistic expectations about the people you meet. You are likely going to date several people who don't work out. Statistics tell us that many of those you meet will be people you never want to see again. Others won't want to see you again!

Don't be discouraged if things don't work out. Recognize that part of the experience is the journey. You're meeting people and finding out what works for you and what doesn't. If the next person has the same qualities you liked in the first, but likes you, too, you're onto something.

It's best to be reasonable about long distance relationships from the beginning. Are you willing to commit to flying across the country every week? Driving 50 miles and back several times a week? It can be done, but be sure you are really prepared to make that commitment.

Take it slowly. Sometimes we think we know someone because we've connected online, but we don't really know him at that point. Don't agree to something unwise, like going on a cruise with someone you've never met.

Be yourself. Computer dating is not the place to present a new you or try to reinvent who you are. It's the time to find someone with whom the real you can connect over the long term.

Online Dating Mistakes

You've gone and done it. You've looked over the online dating services and finally decided to take the plunge. When you've gone looking for an online singles place you realize that there are so many to choose from and it's not an easy decision. After rejecting the ones that aren't local, the ones that are downright creepy and the ones where you get a bad vibe when they keep asking for your credit card, you settle on one that seems to fit you just right. After you filled out all their questionnaires and gave them your photo you sat back and waited for your mailbox to fill up.

It's ok because your potential dates don't get your real email, the email is forwarded from the dating service, which gives you an added level of security, knowing that someone you don't like won't be able to really find you and harass you.

So you began getting a few tentative hi's and hey there's and you've looked at the profiles of those who have responded and perhaps you've even reached out and made the first move on someone whose profile you found intriguing.

You get a bunch of hits from many good-looking men on your site in the dating personals. Okay, so they aren't all models, but the first mistake you can make is writing someone off based on your own feelings of inadequacy. You notice that his teeth are a bit yellow, or he is going bald. These are superficial, and if you are that judgmental, you aren't ever going to find the man of your dreams.

In this world of artificial smiles, it's sometimes difficult to tell what's real and what's not. Getting to know someone online before you meet them might be a good way to sift through those that are right for you and those that have a high-creepy factor. Spend as much time as you need online before taking the step of meeting in the real world. If something isn't feeling right in virtual reality, it's not going to feel right in the real world.

Online dating is fun and exciting and can lead to long term relationships in the real world if you're patient, careful and trust your instincts.

Online Dating 101

You're a busy person. You work, you work out, you volunteer at the local animal no-kill shelter and you recycle all your newspapers, plastics and even your yard waste. You're a good person. You help elderly people across busy streets and you always find time to call your parents and make sure they're all right. When you come home at night from a busy day at the office your cat is the only warmth that you cuddle up to and you want something more. How do you fit finding someone special into your busy life?

Online dating services. Sure they once had a bad rap as the only place losers would go to look for love but that's changed a great deal in the past few years. There are many reputable singles and dating services to be found online. Many of these places put you through a rigorous screening in order to allow you to enter their hallowed halls of dating. You can be sure that all the other members there have been put through the same intense scrutiny that you were and have obviously passed the test. There are dating services that cater to the busy professional, college students who are too busy to mix and mingle in person and everything else in between.

Does this mean you should let your guard down? No, of course not. Just as someone can beat a lie detector test, so too can people lie and fool the people giving the online questionnaires. Always trust your instincts and be careful.

That being said, there are a lot of great people who are in the dating pool and are looking for someone as wonderful as you are.

The first thing you need to do is shop for just the right dating service to fit your needs. You can choose a local service or a global one. Once you decide on the dating service you want, fill out their paperwork and then go looking around to see what they have to offer. And you can do this all from the privacy and comfort of your own home and on your own time.

Online Dating Advice For Women: The Online Personal Ad

Do you think that online dating is only for nerds or misfits? Think again. It's estimated that over 8 million men visit online dating sites every month looking for their perfect match. That comes out to an average of 267,000 men every day.

The internet is changing many aspects of the past as we know it and one of those is dating. Online dating services have become the latest and greatest craze, with both men and women rushing to the web to find their "matches" or read their admirors's emails via an internet connection rather than communicating in the old-fashioned upfront and personal way.

Online sources like eHarmony and Lavalife boast that they "match up" happy couples so successfully that many of them promise a match within six months of joining their services. The following online dating advice for women will start from the beginning. . .how to create your first online personal ad.

The first concept you need to grasp in creating your personal ad is that you will have a lot of competition. So you need to make sure that you stand out from the crowd. You want to be unique and as specific as possible. Also, if you can establish a sense of urgency, that's an extra added touch. This means conveying a message that you will not be around waiting forever.

Think of your personal ad as a sales page. . .for yourself. So, you'll have a headline, your personal profile and a close which guarantees the "sale".

Start with the headline. This is the most important part so make it good. Studies have shown you have three seconds to capture the attention of whoever is reading your headline. A great way to do this is to ask a question. . .something that gets the reader to think.

The next step is your profile. This is where many women need this online dating advice for women because they get this part wrong. In the profile, you will write about what you do and don't like, your activities, etc. Anyone can say that they like reading, traveling, swimming, etc. Instead, write in detail about one of your favorite places or a place that you are planning to visit in the near future. This stimulates your next date's senses.

In the close of your profile, let your readers know that you will be off again soon (maybe to one of those interesting places you mentioned in your profile).

Here are a couple of general points to keep in mind when preparing your profile. Make sure it is grammatically correct. If it isn't, you will appear either stupid or lazy. Next, only three+ out of every 10 women who post a personal ad on a dating site get a response. This is because most women's ads are boring, repetitive or filled with errors.

Best Dating Website - Tips For Finding the Best
The internet is filled with all kinds of websites for finding dating partners. With so many of them out there, it can be tricky to find the best dating website or sites that are right for you. Here are some things to consider when trying to select the best ones.

If you have any friends or family that have used dating sites, then ask them about their personal experiences with different sites; good and bad. This is a good way to get started because these people have a good idea of who you are as a person, and can offer specifics that they find relevant to you.

Next, if part of your self-identity is based on being a member of a particular group, you may wish to see if there are any dating websites that cater to it. There are dating sites that are based on race, religion, orientation, location, and much more. Such sites can get quite specific and may be a good match for you.

Once you have it narrowed down to a few it's time to look into the site itself to see if it qualifies as a best dating website. Go through the following checklist for each site you are thinking about.

1) Number of members. For the most part, the more members a site has, the more people you will have to choose from. And more people means a better chance of finding a match you're happy with. However, this shouldn't be the only consideration as the quality of the membership is more important than the quantity.

2) Safety. What steps does the website take to ensure the safety of its members? Granted, they can't protect you from yourself, but there should be some things in place to keep people safe.

3) Privacy. This goes hand-in-hand with safety. Let's face it, while most people are honest, there are enough weirdos out there to be cautious. The best dating websites have procedures in place whereby members can contact one another without revealing any personal information; such as email address, telephone number and where you live. See if you will be able to communicate via email or chat by using an account that is set up through the site, and only used on the site.

4) Encouragement. This can come in many forms, but the basic idea is that the site does things to encourage people to make matches. Online events, dating guides and tips for writing a better profile (one which is likely to get more responses) are a few examples.

5) Value. The price of membership can vary wildly between sites, but how much you pay isn't nearly as important as how much value you get for your money. You can't put a price on finding the right person for you, but you also don't want to throw your money away. The best dating website will have the things you need and satisfy the elements on this checklist.

I recommend the following internet dating sites to meet men:

1. Zoosk - This is a Premier dating app for casual & serious relationships
2. EliteSingles - This is a Serious online dating for single professionals
3. eharmony - You can connect with quality people seeking long-term commitment
4. SilverSingles - This is for singles 50+ looking for romance & companionship
5. Stir - This Dating site made just for single parents
6. Match - You will be matched with singles based on true compatibility

7. OurTime - You can meet mature singles near you with similar interests
8. BlackPeopleMeet - This is a dating network for Black singles looking to connect
9. Jdate - This is a Premium dating site for Jewish singles
10. BeNaughty - This is a casual dating site for fun, like-minded people

Find Your Perfect Match With Christian Online Dating

Any Christian in the singles world knows that it can be very difficult to find other Christians to date. Thousands of single Christians are turning to Christian Online Dating to help in the process.

The stereotypical way to meet other singles to date is to go to a bar. However, many Christians don't want to visit bars. They're often not interested in the kinds of people they'd meet at a bar. Christian online dating helps them bypass the wilder singles scene and find people compatible with their lifestyle.

If you live in a large city, there are so many people around, that it is difficult to find out enough about them before asking them out. It is not always obvious who values their Christian faith. In these cases, the online option can help you find people within your city who want to date other Christians.

In smaller cities, rural or suburban areas, it may be even more difficult to find potential partners. Singles in these areas depend even more on Christian online dating to find other singles following the Christian path. There are more and more people using these online services.

The greatest benefit for those who use Christian online dating services is that the singles know immediately that they have shared values. It is possible to look at profiles of potential dates and see what their commitment level is. People can screen for denomination, desire for service, tithing habits, etc. to find those truly compatible.

This kind of online matching gives Christian singles a great way to expand their social circles. They often offer opportunities for spiritual growth as well. Those who are registered on sites can join Bible discussion groups, for example.

Not only are these a great way to add to their scriptural knowledge, but they are also a great way to get to know other singles. Reading interactions in a chat room can be like having an initial conversation. You see what things are important, how the person interacts with others, and if they share your beliefs and understandings.

There are services that cater to specific denominations. For some Christians, finding a dating or socializing partner of the same faith is important. For these people, denomination specific sites are a great idea.

It's important to choose the right service; one that has compatible values. Examine the terms of use, also. See what they require upfront, and how many Christians from your local area use the service. Most services offer a free trial period, so you can find out how many others from the area are involved before you join officially.

The prices for such services are generally modest. A month's membership will cost about what a night out costs. For many, the much-simplified process of finding Christians with whom they can socialize offsets the cost of the services.

If you want to find Christians to date, but have trouble knowing where to look, Christian online dating may be the answer for you.

Find Love on Christian Dating Sites

Seeking companionship does not have to be difficult, if you begin your search on one of many online Christian dating sites. Matchmaking services and dating services have been available for many years now, attempting to make the search for companionship simpler than ever before. Now, not only are there a myriad of dating sites available, but there are also specialized dating sites that are designed for the needs of specific groups of people.

One example of this is Christian dating sites, which are designed to cater to people following a Christian faith who are looking to meet other singles from the same faith. Christian dating sites are one of many unique dating sites designed to cater to a specific group of people. By catering to Christians and followers of similar faiths, these dating sites make it easier to meet people that share similar beliefs. If your belief system is important, then choosing a site that helps you meet people with similar faith is essential.
Rather than wading through dating sites wondering if the people you will meet are going to have the same core beliefs, joining Christian dating sites will allow you to know that every profile that you view, and every person that you meet will share the same Christian views that you hold dear, and this is a vital part of making a Christian relationship work. In other words, Christian dating sites are ideal for anyone who is serious about their faith, and who wants to meet up with other people who are serious about their faith and beliefs as well. Choosing a dating site that is dedicated to Christianity will allow you to meet people that have core beliefs in common with you.

This is a great way to forge a brand new relationship because you already will know that you agree when it comes to religion and spirituality. It would be a shame to fall in love with someone, only to find out that they do not have the same religious beliefs as you. Christian dating sites, however, help to assure you that everyone you meet will share the same beliefs, and religious beliefs are important when it comes to forging new relationships.

If you want to get it right the first time when choosing dating sites and meeting people online, then you need to be willing to find a site that will offer you the right results. Not every dating site is going to connect you with the right eligible singles, so it would be wise for you to shop around and pick the most ideal dating site for your needs. Christian dating sites are an outstanding place for you to meet people online if your Christian faith is important to you and you want to meet someone that shares the same level of belief as you do.

Spice Up Your Love Life With Christian Dating Services

Think that Christian dating organizations are filled with boring people who are not really all that interested in anything but God? Wondering what Christian dating services can do to spice up your love life? Well, studies show that the most interesting people, as well as the most trustworthy people, report having a deep faith in Jesus, so if you are looking to enjoy a great relationship, a faith based dating service should be the first place you look for love, not the last.

A Christian dating service can spice up your love life by helping you find the perfect person who holds the same interests and beliefs that are important to you; everything is better when you find the one you were meant to be with, and let's face it, a long-lasting relationship needs more than just physical attraction to last. The Christian relationship match up service can help you find someone who is more than just a pretty face. They can help you locate someone with the same values as yours.

In addition, faith based relationship services can spice up your love life by taking into account all the different aspects of both your life and the lives of your potential matches. Although the little things in life do indeed affect your everyday life, it is important not to lose sight of the really important things, too, like your faith. Using a faith dating service ensures that you and your match already share the most fundamental and important aspect of life: your trust and faith in Christ.

Not only that, but Christian dating services can also help with practical daily issues that you encounter in both the dating world and the rest of the world, as well. For example, Christ believing dating services can save you time. Why spend several weeks getting to know someone, feeling as if he might be the one you have been searching for, and then find out he or she doesn't believe in God? You know that will never work out, and you just wasted weeks of time, when you could have been assured of his/her fundamental beliefs right from the start.

Under that same scenario, using a Christian dating service would have also saved you some emotional turmoil. I mean, beginning to fall for someone and then having to break it off can be heartbreaking, right? Who needs it? If you happen to be the male half of the equation (or a modern Millie), that same scenario also probably costs a bit of money, too, which means that there will be less to spend when you do actually find that perfect girl. Why not avoid that whole thing and skip right to the proper source for finding a true Christian love?

The next time you decide that you are ready to forge a head in your search for your soul mate and a little spice in your love life, you would be well advised to start with a service that can ensure the most important part of your life is shared by your potential partner.

P.S. I highly recommend this website to meet Christian men: www.christianmingle.com -You are Christian. You're single. Find God's soul mate for you at Christian Mingle. Make a meaningful lifelong connection with someone who shares your beliefs!

Chapter 4 - How to Meet Women Using Personal Ads

This section is devoted to the highly effective way of meeting men by answering and running personal classified ads in national and local singles publications. Many women have used this method and get stacks of letters (with photos) or emails from lovely men from all over the United States and locally.

There are lots of lonely men out there searching for romance and companionship. Advertising is a dignified way for them to meet women and they are able to screen the women that respond through their letters, photos, emails, and phone calls.

There's only going to be one drawback to this method unless you meet someone local. You will probably have to do some traveling to meet the men and this could become an expensive habit. It's well worth it if you can afford it. A lot of people have found their life mate this way. If you like to travel, you can travel all over the U.S. meeting men you've become intimate with through correspondence, emails, and talking over the phone.

Some men will even visit you from out of state as they did me. Some even paid for all their expenses. I really had some fun times!

How to Get Men to Write You First

This involves running a good pulling ad in the several good national publications. Always keep at least one ad running at all times.

Let's talk about running a good ad that will "pull." Whatever you do, don't publish a short ad with basic information about yourself. This won't work and you'll receive very few replies from such an uninteresting and plain, dull ad.

Your ad's got to appeal to men. You've got to convince him that you're not average and have a lot to offer him. You've got to offer him something he can't get from the average woman. You've really got to interest him to answer your ad.

Here's an example of a national ad that was very successful for me and you could use for internet dating sites also:

I LOVE YOU DARLING! How long have you longed to hear these words? How often have you longed to be held in a woman's arms, to be cuddled, caressed and kissed, warmly, sweetly, tenderly? Perhaps you are my sweetheart - who knows? Nice, attractive one-man woman, writer, author, publisher, 35, 5'1", 100 lbs., desires to meet attractive, loving, slender man 20-40 who is interested in a meaningful relationship leading to marriage. Photo please.

In summation, include these items in your ad:

1. Occupation.

2. Age, height, and weight.
3. What you're looking for in a man.
4. Age range of men you desire to meet.
5. Your hobbies, interests, and things you like to do.
6. Let him know you are a "one-man woman."
7. You are interested in a meaningful relationship.

The following are some good-pulling ads that have run in some local publications which would work great for internet dating sites also:
This is my favorite! Just run this ad and edit it to fit your description. You will get a lot of replies!

Single female 1993 model, low mileage, high performance. Bumped a few times, but never wrecked. Proven ability to hug the road and not wander off course. Exterior in mint condition, warm, sentimental, sensitive interior, never soiled. Factory equipped entertainment package includes stereo, humor, depth, imagination and intelligence. Radio picks up all kinds of rock and country music. Spacious seats with plenty of room for passenger...runs on high-octane fun and romance, lifetime supply included. Available for inspection by male drivers only, prefer 25-40 eye-catching exterior, self-confident, affectionate, warm, sincere with a sense of humor and full set of tools. Come from a close, solid family, and would like to have little Toyotas some day. Equipped with a . Marketing Degree. Only driven once a week by a little old lady to and from church. To arrange a test drive, please respond. HAPPY MOTORING.

Here are some cute ads I found in various local singles publications:

SWF, 34, very attractive, slender hot potato, recently dropped, needs to be rescued by an unattached male who needs permanent outside diversion. No monetary obligation.

SWMF, 30, very attractive, slender Catholic needs a mature church-going male (25-40, attractive, slender) for a lasting and loving relationship. Must be into group functions, wafers, and early morning mass.

SWF, 28, very attractive, slender, who flunked Disco and Bars 101, seeking attractive, slender, affectionate male (25-40), for the usual reasons.

SWF, very attractive, affectionate, with nice body, 25, needs male companionship (20-30, attractive, romantic, and slender) for movie going, dancing, warm friendship and finishing all my leftovers.

SWF, 34, nice-looking, slender, would like to meet a male of the same marital status (25-45, handsome, slender) for "war story" exchange and soothing battle scars.

Final tip. Don't list your name, address, or phone number in an ad. This will give the impression that you're desperate and undesirable.

Here's a list of good national publications to post your ad:

The Sheela Wood personals section offers thousands of Globe and National Examiner readers every week a favorite way to find love, friendship, pen pals and former classmates.

Countless friendships and relationships have been realized through the Sheela Wood personals section. When you place your listing in Sheela Wood, it will be published in both the Globe and National Examiner. Two popular publications, one low price!

These two publications are at all your local grocery stores, department stores, etc.

For more information and to place a personal ad please visit: **www.russelljohns.com/pubs/sheela-wood** or just google: sheela wood personals

Here are some more places to place your personal ad:

Reddit (spelled r_e_d_d_i_t) Personals at: www.reddit.com/r/r4r - You can simply make your own ad here, let men know about yourself and what you're looking for, and see if you get any kind of response. As Reddit is free, it's pretty much a no-lose option.

Locanto (spelled L_o_c_a_n_t_o) at www.locanto.com - You can post a personal ad to let men know what it is exactly that you're hoping to find.

Tinder at: www.tinder.com - Tinder likely doesn't need a whole lot of introduction, as it's become one of the most popular "dating" apps around. There's a basic free version as well as a paid tier called Tinder Gold that gives you extra features and unlimited swiping.

Pernals (spelled p_e_r_n_a_l_s) at: www.pernals.com - Pernals gives you the opportunity to create your own personal ad for free. This means you can put exactly what you're looking for, whether that's a serious relationship, casual hookup, even a friend, etc.

Bedpage at: www.bedpage.com - It has the same types of categories as Craigslist Personals: women seeking men, men seeking women, etc.

Classified Ads at: www.classifiedads.com - Simply select "Personals" on the front page and you'll see the classic categories.

OkCupid at: www.okcupid.com - It doesn't require a paid membership in order to look for matches or message people. That said, like most dating sites nowadays, you may be tempted to pay in order to unlock certain features.

Harvard Magazine at: www.harvardmagazine.com - Go to classifieds and post an ad to the personals section.

Animal Lovers Personals at: www.animalpeople.com - For meeting men who love animals and want to meet women with similar interests.

Signal Penpal Magazine at: www.signalpenpals.net - Meet and write to men all over the world. Your listing is FREE!

The main thing is that you use good judgment and stay safe. A lot of sites are loaded with scammers looking to take advantage of lonely people. It's sad, yes, but true. Remember to follow basic common sense and never send anyone personal information or money before you've actually met them and verified that everything is legitimate. If you're ever in doubt, you should probably recognize that and listen to your gut!

When the Man Answers Your Ad

The main objective in responding to his letter or email is to make a good impression on him.

When using a letter to respond to an ad, don't write back on cheap ordinary writing paper.

You've got to use first class elegant stationery. Ivory and blue colors look real nice with matching envelopes.

If you have illegible handwriting, you'll make a better impression by typing the letter. If you don't type, you can hire a secretarial service to type it out for you or have a friend do it for you.

Your Letter

Here's the actual letter I used to write back to the men that answered my national ad in Sheela Wood Personals. This letter was very successful and I got a lot of positive responses with it. Modify it to fit your situation.

Dear Don:

Thank you for answering my ad in "Globe Magazine." I really appreciated your lovely photo. On the basis of your "sweet" letter and photo, I've come to the conclusion that you are a very nice person and the type of man I've been looking for. I sincerely hope we get a chance to meet, for I feel that a man like you could make my life happy in many ways. My main goal in life at this time is to meet an unmarried and unattached man who is sincerely interested in marriage to a one-man woman. I'm not concerned about your religion or economic status as these things are unimportant to me. What is important to me are your truthfulness, honesty, and loyalty. If married to you, I will share all the wealth I've accumulated in the past and future on an equal basis. As my husband, lover and friend, everything is half yours and I am a very unselfish person.

I'm white, single, educated, refined, generous, well-informed on all subjects, intelligent, attractive, well-groomed, and have a good sense of humor. I know how to treat a man and I know I could satisfy and fulfill your needs like you've never experienced before.

I'm extremely affectionate and very romantic. I love candlelight dinners, fireplaces, holding hands, walking hand in hand along the beach at sunset, and bubble baths. Also, I love to shower the "man in my life" with lots of kisses and tokens of affection such as flowers, cards, gifts, etc. I will accept you as you are and would not try to change you. I think it's very important for a man to be "himself." I would want to expand your life and not try to suppress it in any manner. I'm not the jealous, domineering, and possessive type at all. If married to me you would remain independent and could pursue and enjoy all the activities that you enjoy. Also, if married to me you would know of my whereabouts and what I was doing at all times. I love traveling and taking many long trips. As my husband you would become my traveling companion. I have been to 43 states and 10 foreign countries. There's nothing I wouldn't enjoy more than seeing interesting places with the man I love.

I'm a very modern woman in all respects and very up-to-date with the times. I don't live in the past and live one day at a time with a positive outlook.

My leisure activities include mountain-climbing, canoeing, kayaking, fishing, camping, hiking, and bowling, playing the organ and guitar, and all sports. Also, I enjoy eating out, good music of all kinds, live theater, reading, going to movies, and good conversation.

Your physical looks are not of the utmost importance to me. I'm more interested in "inner beauty." I'll take a warm-hearted plain-looking man any day over a handsome guy with a cold heart. I'll have to admit that it is nice to have a very attractive man to look at, but physical beauty is an attribute that fades with age, giving way to wrinkles and added weight.

In case you're wondering why I answered your ad. Well it can be summed up in Johnny Lee's hit song, "Looking For Love in All the Wrong Places." In the past I've gone to nightclubs to meet the opposite sex. All I've gotten out of this is shallow relationships and the all too common, "one night stand." The men I meet don't seem to be interested in a meaningful relationship. They just want to play the field. I just can't handle all the game playing in clubs. That's why I wrote to you. At least I know you're looking for a meaningful relationship and someone to love just as I am.

I am very easygoing and easy to please. I also believe in sharing responsibilities on an equal basis. I love to cook. I'd share all the domestic chores with you and I'm no perfectionist when it comes to housecleaning.

I must be totally honest with you and tell you that I consider sex very important in marriage. I have a strong, passionate, and healthy sex drive. It would be important to me that you have a healthy attitude towards sex have a desire to keep your woman satisfied and fulfilled in this important area. Concerning children, if you desired to have children that would be OK with me. If you didn't desire to have children that would be OK also. I'd be happy with you with or without children.

If you're still interested, Don, I would like to hear from you again real soon. At the bottom of this letter you will find my home and business phone numbers. Feel free to call me anytime. Please tell me about yourself, the things you enjoy, your goals in life, and anything you have strong feelings about. This would be helpful to evaluate the things we have in common and if we could get along in a close relationship (marriage).

I have a lot to offer you as a wife, lover, and friend and if you're interested, I would like for us to meet and spend some time together to determine if we are compatible and if we could become deeply involved in a relationship. If this worked out favorably and we hit it off really well, I would favor us getting married soon. Being that distance separates us, it would be difficult to have a long courtship involving numerous trips and dates. A conventional courtship would definitely be out of the question.

So if you're disappointed and tired of what you've had up till now and want to settle down, and ready for a first-class woman to come into your life and treat you like a King and fill your life with love and happiness, please write or call me without further delay. If you can recognize a truly sincere letter, then you'll know that this is "the real thing."

Sincerely, Susan

You Write the Men First

All you do is read through the personal ads and circle the ones that appeal to you. Then you will answer with your printed form letter or by email.

This is a quick way to get those letters or emails and photos to start coming in. You don't even have to wait for any ads to break.

You're going to be using a printed form letter rather than answering letters by hand. Writing letters would be too time consuming.

You will find that a lot of these men are sincerely interested in a meaningful relationship. A lot of them live in remote areas where there aren't too many eligible women to choose from. Of course there's the type out there that are just looking for a free meal ticket and a rich woman. But, most of them are sincere and nice men.

Some words of advice. Don't answer ads where they don't list their weight. They are usually overweight. If obesity doesn't bother you, then answer anyway. Also, if no age is listed they are usually too old for you. Stay away from recently divorced men also. They are a poor prospect for a relationship due to their emotionally unstable state of mind.

OK, now you're ready to answer an ad. Don't send a photo to a blind ad. They are expensive and some will not answer your letter back and you'll be minus a photo. Don't send a photo until he writes you a nice encouraging letter containing his photo. Then send him one. There's one exception concerning photos. If you are good-looking, I'd recommend sending a photo initially. This will increase your chances of him responding. This option is up to you.

Follow the publications directions carefully when answering ads.

Here's a sample of a form letter I used when answering national ads:

Hi!

I LOVE YOU DARLING! How often have you longed to hear these words? How often have you longed to be held in the arms of a woman who is affectionate and loving, to be cuddled, caressed and kissed, warmly, sweetly, tenderly?   Perhaps you are my sweetheart - who knows?

This letter is in response to your recent "personal" ad.

I'm 5'1", 100 lbs. Professionally I'm a writer, published author, professional astrologer, and own my own publishing company. Also, I've been an industrial lab technician for over 14 years. As you can tell, I'm very ambitious and one of my main goals in life is to become financially independent. I am now and have been taking steps to fulfill that goal.

I desire to meet an unmarried and unattached man who is sincerely interested in marriage to a one-woman man. Your religion and economic status are really not important to me. Your honesty, truthfulness, and loyalty are of utmost importance to me. If married to me you could pursue your own career, but if for some reason you didn't want to I would prefer that you help me run our business operations, but again this would not be required if you didn't want to. If married to you, I would, of course, share what I've accumulated in the past, plus what I earn and accumulate in the future on an equal basis with you. I'm a very unselfish person and as my husband, lover and "lifetime" companion I would truly consider everything half yours. I'm white (German, French, and Irish), educated, intelligent well-informed, good sense of humor, clean, neat dresser, beautiful teeth, age 35 (look much younger), very attractive (been told many times that I look like a model), extremely affectionate and romantic, refined and generous. I'm modern up-to-date and in-step with the times, and not trying to relive or hold on to the past.

I do not smoke but have no objections to the man in my life smoking. It is important to me that he "be himself," so I have no desire to try and take away any of those things that you already have that are valuable and important to you. I would want to enhance and expand your life, and not suppress it in any manner. This is what love is all about. I would want you happy as my spouse and I feel that those things I advocate here would be necessary for total happiness. I'm not the jealous type of person. If married to me you certainly would not lose your independence, and therefore you could "be yourself" and pursue those activities in which you are interested.

All the things I like to do for recreation, I like to do them with the "man in my life." I drink an occasional mixed drink and I enjoy two or three drinks in the evening when out with my lover. If married to me you would know of my whereabouts and what I was doing at all times.

I have two nice color TV'S in my home, but seldom ever turn them on. The normal shows on TV bore me to death. I prefer reading when at home in the evening unless there's a good "special" on TV or sports. I keep up with current events by reading the paper and listening to radio news. I very much enjoy going on long trips to interesting places and doing interesting things with the man in my life. I have been to 26 states and 10 foreign countries.

I am not interested in "one night stands" with men. I could never exploit and use men in this manner, knowing full well that I had no future to offer them. Sweet and lovely guys are too "precious" to me for me to ever exploit and use them. I'm looking for a meaningful and lasting relationship with one man that will lead to early marriage.

I'm mature and well-established. Your age is unimportant to me if you are sincere, and mature in your thinking. As you know, age does not always denote the degree of maturity in one's thinking. Your physical looks are not of primary importance to me as long as you're clean and neat in appearance. While it is nice to have someone who is nice to look at, physical beauty is a fleeting thing and fades with age, invariably giving way to "father time." I'm far more interested in "inner beauty", love, respect and admiration for each other that is not affected by time, and can and should last forever.

My leisure activities include mountain-climbing, canoeing, kayaking, fishing, camping, hiking, and bowling, playing the organ and guitar, and all sports. I might add that I am a fitness nut also. Also, I enjoy dining out, good music of all kinds, love to dance, live theater, reading, going to the movies and good conversation.

I love candlelight dinners, fireplaces, holding hands while walking along the beach at sunset, bubble baths, and giving back rubs. Also, I love to shower "the man in my life" with lots of kisses and tokens of affection such as flowers, cards, gifts, etc.

I'm as down-to-earth as an "old shoe", so please realize that what I need from you is certainly nothing complicated. I realize that all of the desirable characteristics, traits and talents will never be found all combined in one man. Neither will they all be found in one woman. We all have our faults, and to me the sensible thing to do is decide what is important to us in our partner, and when we find these things be ready to accept our good fortune, and be ready to accept and be happy with those shortcomings that are of lesser importance.

I'm no fanatic on housekeeping, and when married I try to share these chores on somewhat of a 50-50 basis with my spouse, because after all, I live there too.

It is important to me that my husband, lover and companion try to be a good sex partner. I'm very feminine and normal in this area. This part of a marriage is very valuable to me and I would be less than honest with you if I didn't tell you so. I don't expect any outstanding performances, and certainly nothing weird. The important thing to me is a good attitude in wanting to keep her woman satisfied and happy.

If we were married and you wanted children this would be OK with me. On the other hand, if you didn't want children this would be OK too. I could be happy with you either way.

If you're interested and are unmarried and truly unattached (not still in love with another woman), then I would like to hear from you soon. I would appreciate receiving a recent photo from you. I will answer without delay. Please tell me about anything you have strong feelings about, and any activities which you are deeply involved in. This would help me determine if I feel I could adjust to your lifestyle in a close relationship (marriage).

If you're interested in what I have to offer as a wife, lover, provider and lifetime companion, I would like for us to get together soon and spend some time together to check things out for compatibility, and determine if we feel we could develop a deep love for each other. If this resulted in working things out to the mutual satisfaction of both of us I would favor getting married without a lot of additional delay. The distance that separates us makes it impractical for us to conduct a long courtship with a lot of long trips and dates. The conventional courtship is out of the question.

If we did get married it would be necessary for you to relocate to Houston. My wanting you to do the relocation is not a selfish motive on my part. The fact is it would be extremely difficult for me to relocate my business operations and ever get them re-- established and profitable.

So, if you're tired of and disappointed in what you've had up to now, and tired of working (maybe caught up in a "treadmill to nowhere" type of job), and are ready for a first class woman to come into your life and extend to you first class treatment, please write me without further delay. If you can recognize a sincere letter, then you know that this is the "real thing."

Affectionately, Susan

Here's a sample letter or email to use when answering local ads or non local ads:

Hi!

I LOVE YOU DARLING! How often have you longed to hear these words? How often have you longed to be held in your arms by a woman who is loving and affectionate - to be cuddled, caressed and kissed, warmly, sweetly, tenderly? Perhaps you are my sweetheart - who knows?

This letter is in response to your recent "personal" ad. A little bit about me:

WHAT I LIKE TO DO: I love sad movies with happy endings and happy movies with no endings. Have been known to wander the beach late at night just to see the moonlight playing on the water...Addicted to the horse races in Louisiana, the French Quarter, and tubing down the river drinking margaritas...My leisure activities include mountain-climbing, canoeing, fishing, camping, hiking, bowling, playing the organ and guitar, reading, and I love all sports...I love poetry, books, walks on the beach and cozy candlelight dinners (I'll do the cooking). I enjoy movies, love live comedy theater, all kinds of music (I love to dance), the desert, the quietness of the mountains, the ocean, sunrises and sunsets, and dining out.

WHO I AM: I have never been a game player. I never want personal happiness at the expense of someone else.

If we have a single date or a lifetime together, I will never lie to you, try to manipulate you or use you in any way. I am an incurable romantic who treasures, cherishes and appreciates sincerity, integrity, honesty and warmth. I enjoy picnics, laughing, talking, touching, affection and physical closeness. A good listener who enjoys mutual spoiling...I'm a person who feels a oneness with the earth, who is in tune with nature, who loves the outdoors, and all things bright and beautiful that the earth has to offer, including rainbows, waterfalls, bluebonnet fields, moon and stars, mountains, the ocean, and animals... Also, I have a very positive attitude and I'm a goal-oriented person. I know where I'm going in life and how to get there.

WHAT I AM LOOKING FOR: LET'S BECOME GOOD FRIENDS, then...HOPE FOR A VERY BEAUTIFUL RELATIONSHIP. I feel that before we can have a good relationship, we must put forth the energy and time it takes to first become good friends. Friendship is one of the most important building blocks of a good relationship. To me, friends are like flowers in the garden of life...I am looking for a special, loving relationship with a unique man who is affectionate, attractive, slender, with a nice physique, sincere, easygoing, with interests and characteristics similar to mine - someone who wants a meaningful, serious, long-term relationship - not just a few dates. Are you that special man?...I am interested in a man who needs love, tenderness, sympathetic understanding, to share a long-lasting relationship with a one-man woman.

So, if you're disappointed in what you've had up until now and ready for a first class woman to come into your life and extend to you first class treatment, please get in touch with me without further delay. Contact me today. Do it now!

Sincerely, Susan

A final word of advice. If you live in an apartment, list your address as a suite number rather than an apartment number. This creates the impression that you are well-to-do and live in a high-rise penthouse. Also, if you're concerned about proposing marriage in a letter, don't worry about it. This is just used to attract men and show them that you mean business. You're in no way obligated to marry them. Then again, you may meet the man of your dreams.

Chapter 5 - How and Where to Meet Well-to-Do Men

First off, remember women, you don't have to be a "10." This chapter isn't about the numbers game, so I'm not going to waste your time telling you how to be what some narrow-minded men think you should look like in their eyes. What you have to offer a well-to-do man are YOU along with your attributes and faults. Don't offer a phony cover up or pat conversation. For example, if a man says he likes a particular hobby, lifestyle or whatever and it goes against everything you've always believed, it would be deceptive for you to tell him it's always been your favorite too, just for the sake of appearing to be the one for him. This whole idea most often backfires along the way, leaving the man feeling betrayed and seriously jeopardizing your future credibility. When you meet these well-to-do men, above all be yourself!

This is not to say you shouldn't make an effort to improve yourself. Wear appropriate clothing when you are out meeting these men. Don't overdress, as you will stand out in a way that won't help your cause. If you're asked to a formal dinner, if at all possible, find out what the other women are planning to wear. If necessary, you can call the place where the dinner will be and ask the maitre d' what the women wear. If you're not certain what is proper etiquette, look around you and follow suit. If you're alone with the man and you're not certain what drink to order or you don't understand the menu, ask him to suggest something or to surprise you. Also, you could tell him that you don't understand the menu and ask him to suggest something. Tell him you don't drink much and what would he recommend.

One of the cardinal rules in your search for the well-to-do man is to forget the bars. The person you're looking for isn't wasting time in them. You have to go where the rich and soon to be rich spend their time. If you like boating and water, many yacht clubs allow people to join on social status who don't even own boats. What better way to meet a well-to-do man than to be a member of this club and be present at the various social functions the club provides. This allows you to mingle with a lot of people of means without having a large cash outlay yourself.

If you're a horse lover, find an exclusive stable or riding club and join up. This doesn't mean you have to have a horse of your own to learn to ride.

If you can afford the membership dues in a country club or if you can afford to borrow the money to join up, do so. If you are an aspiring golfer, most areas have places you can even rent the clubs. On public courses without restrictions make sure you're playing during the middle of the week whenever possible. It's a common joke your doctors and lawyers are on the course during this time. Usually they play the country clubs but they have been known to play on public courses. Better supermarkets are excellent meeting places for the upwardly mobile, as are better department stores. You can be working there or shopping there, just as long as these eligible men see you. Some of the really large stores such as Bloomies in New York have entire departments devoted to party needs such as wine, cheese, crackers or hors d'oeuvre s, etc. Want to meet a nice on-the-way up type of man; He's here buying for a fun party. It's a sure bet if you're looking around this type of party center, conversation will develop if you let it or even better, start it.

In University towns, the libraries are excellent meeting places for soon to be lawyers and doctors and other assorted professional types. Ideally, you should be in the University library as opposed to the public one. This could necessitate enrolling in one course to get the card entitling you to use the library. Take something fun and easy.

There are loads of opportunities to meet eligible, well-to-do men while working as dental assistants, receptionists to doctors and attorneys, businessmen and the like. The pay isn't always the highest but it affords you the opportunity to meet a lot of different people including male executives, etc. Salesmen in prestigious car dealerships like Mercedes, Cadillac, etc. meet a lot of well-to-do men looking for cars and maybe you. There's also the opportunity here to make a good living.

Real estate is always a good avenue to follow in pursuit of a good career and chances to meet well-to-do men. You will meet successful men looking to buy a home. The economy is currently not as generous to realtors as it once was but this too will pass. For the moment, get to night school and get that realtors license so you'll be ready to meet those men looking for a home when that market starts to loosen up.

Airline stewardesses meet a great many successful men. Airline ticket persons meet the same people but usually don't have the time to start a relationship because of the lines and the need to get these people out. A stewardess can get more exposure to the well-to-do passenger and perhaps start a relationship that will continue after the plane has landed.

Top waitresses in better restaurants meet a lot of successful types who would love to get married and take care of you in a style you'd love to get accustomed to. Female hair stylists in styling salons and other types of women's beauty care centers will invariably meet the well-to-do men.

The basic idea behind meeting a well-to-do man is to be where they are in one capacity or another. If they see you with a certain amount of frequency, things will take their natural course. You will never meet them at work if you work on an assembly line, in a women's clothing store or as a telephone operator. In short, you need exposure either at work or at one of the previously mentioned clubs, golf courses, etc. The more familiar you become to them as when you're seen in their office, club, hair salon, barbershop, etc., day after day, the better. The most important single thing is for YOU to be seen by them. Familiarity breeds relationships! Good luck, women.

Chapter 6 - How to Meet Flight Attendants

Handsome and friendly flight attendants. Go to the concourses of any of the world's airports and you can see them walking in the airport. These are men of mystery. They are like birds in never ending migration. They have an air of confidence about them and are extremely poised.

This is a very proud and select group of men. After all, they have been screened and selected from literally hundreds of applicants to represent their airlines in this highly competitive industry.

I couldn't think of a worldlier man than a flight attendant. After all, how many ordinary men do you know who may have just had breakfast in Boston and lunch in St. Louis and are about to eat chop suey in San Francisco's Chinatown?

There are more airliners in the sky than ever before in United States history and there's a good chance a hot and sexy flight attendant will be on your flight.

Flight attendants are really ideal for a warm, mature, and perhaps a completely physical affair. Why? Well he's not around very much; he usually is intelligent and outgoing; he can shower you with exotic gifts from afar; and finally, he has friends that are flight attendants also.

Now, let's discuss how, when, and where to meet flight attendants. This may surprise you, but the best place to meet a flight attendant is not in the air, but on the ground. OK, am I telling you not to approach them in the air? No, but you will be much more successful on the ground and I will explain why and where to find them later.

Here's how to approach them in the air, if you want to give it a try: After you're in the air and things have calmed down and things are slow, ask the flight attendant for some coffee. Try to establish some eye contact while he's taking your order and be sure and give him a warm and sexy smile. Literally try to melt him with your bedroom eyes and tell him, "You sure look great today." When he returns with your coffee say, "Being a flight attendant sure is a demanding job isn't it?" This sure could open up an avenue for some prolonged conversation. What you're trying to do is establish as much verbal contact as possible.

After you've finished your coffee, call him to pick up your cup. This is when you're going to "move in for the kill." Ask him, "Would it be possible to talk to you in private?" He will probably respond with, "About what?" Just say it's personal. Whether you get to talk to him in private or while in your seat, this is the approach to use: "I'm very attracted to you and I'd like to get to know you better. Can we have dinner or a couple of drinks together?" That's all there is to it and hopefully he will say "yes." If he doesn't, you can't say you didn't try.

Also, if you don't get to speak to him in private and you have to speak to him from your seat and you're sensitive about other passengers listening in on your lines, just have him put his ear down to your mouth and whisper in his ear.

You might try this if you get turned down for dinner or drinks. When you're getting off the plane, be sure and say on your way out, "Are you sure you still don't want to have dinner or a couple of drinks?" You never know, he just might change his mind.

In conclusion to approaching flight attendants in the air, be sure and do it at the beginning of the flight. Don't wait until mid-flight or at the end of the flight. The reason for this being that he may be tired or fed up with difficult passengers. So strike early and get a jump on any possible competition.

Now, I will discuss the best place to meet flight attendants, and that's on the ground. Particularly in the bars of hotels that have regular limousine service to and from the local airport.

Where do flight attendants hang out between flights? It may surprise you but usually they stick around the hotels they stay in. You might think they would be out partying till the wee hours between flights. This is just not so and here are reasons for this.

Being a flight attendant is not all glamor. It's a hectic physical schedule and it takes its toll on the body. For example, a flight attendant typically works only a couple of weeks out of a month. He will spend up to six to eight days at a time flying here and there which includes within the United States or internationally. Then he will be off another six to eight days to recuperate his body from jet lag.

When he's working the stretch and he gets off work, he's usually tired and catches a limo for the hotel and then straight to the bar. This is where you want to be to approach him.

OK, now you're in the hotel bar and a couple of flight attendants walk in. By the way, I might mention that flight attendants are usually paired together when staying in hotels. Take your pick of the one you want to approach and approach him. Keep in mind that they are there for a few quick drinks and then it's off to the sack for some shut eye and relaxation. You have approached him and you open up with, "Hi my name is _____Can I join you for some conversation?" In most cases he will say yes. Now you will follow up with your conversational skills. Follow my techniques described in my chapter on conversation. Be sure and don't come on with a lot of B.S. about yourself. Revolve the whole conversation around himself and his interests. Try to avoid talking about his job. This will probably turn him off because it may just seem like one big long drag for them. It certainly won't hurt to sympathize with him about his hectic schedule and duties such as cleaning up air sickness bag overfill.

You're hitting it off really well with this flight attendant now. Hopefully, if he is with another flight attendant, the other attendant will excuse himself to head for the room to get some sleep. Once he's out of sight say, "I have a nice warm bed, clean sheets, and a potent nightcap at my place. So why don't you stay over at my place tonight?" "I'll sleep on the couch and you can have my bed if you like."

Your own your way now to total heaven now, providing he accepts your invitation.

The next morning you'll probably be up early. Don't be surprised if he's a little grumpy and irritable when he gets up in the morning. His body and mind are just depleted from jet lag and being on his feet. Just be warm and affectionate towards him.

When you drop him off at the airport, be sure and give him your business card (if you have one) and your home phone number. This way the next time he is in town he can give you a call if he would like a nice warm bed for the night and some hot romance.

One sad final thought. He may disappear out of your life for long periods of time. Just accept this because it's a fact of life. When you least expect it, he will call and say, "I'm in town on a layover and I'm just dying to see you!" What he probably really wants is some good food, conversation, and intimacy. So why not give it to him, even though it's most likely not going to lead to something serious.

Chapter 7 - Unique Ways to Meet Men

I'm going to describe some very unusual methods of meeting men that can work very successfully for you. To use these is going to take a little courage and a matter of daring to be a little different, but the results are well worth it.

Circular Method

This is what I refer to as the "Circular Method." It's a very unique way of advertising for romance and several nice and attractive men will contact you. What you will be doing is simply putting circulars on windshields of cars in nightclub and singles bars parking lots.

This is how to do it. Have 100 circulars printed at your local print shop. Also, it would be much cheaper to just do this with your computer and print them out as needed. Here's a sample of what to say:

"Single bars are great if you want to stay single. I don't. And I want a man who doesn't either. So, if you'd like to meet and get together and you are disappointed in what you've had up until now and are ready for a first class woman to come into your life and extend to you first class treatment, just send a photo and short note to: (list your email address):"

The upper part of the circular contains a black and white photo of you. The printing is done in large letters so it would stand out and is done on pink paper.

If you don't want to do the distributing yourself, you might consider hiring someone to do it. This could be a friend, teenagers looking for some spending money, etc. Also, if you live in a large city, look in the yellow pages under distributing services. They might be able to help you.

The best time to do this is between 10 and 12 PM when the parking lots are full, preferably on the weekends. What you might consider doing also is leaving some inside the club. Just talk to the manager and get his permission. They usually don't care. Just leave some near the entrance or where you pay to get in. This is what I did.

In conclusion, feel free to use the wording on the sample circular or make up your own. So why not be brave, daring, and different and give it a try. It sure works and what a thrill it will be having your email with responses from the opposite sex.

The Book Method

What I'm about to describe to you is the best way in the world to attract men to you in bars and nightclubs. It's guaranteed to work and never fails! Men will literally flock all over you. You're probably saying to yourself, "That's a bunch of bull."

Let me explain the method. What you're going to be doing is reading in bars and nightclubs. Sounds crazy doesn't it? Now just place yourself in a man's shoes and you see this woman reading a book in a bar. Your curiosity is going to be killing you and you've just got to find out what she's reading and why in a bar. Get the picture now?

This is a highly successful method of attracting attention from men. Some men will even leave their dates to talk to you. You'll have a big edge on the other women because you're doing something unusual and different.

What should I be reading you ask? Well I'd recommend self-improvement, motivational and get rich books.

When you're asked why you're reading, you can go into detail about wanting to improve yourself and you wanting to become financially independent. You tell them you're reading these books to motivate you and improve your life.

OK, now what to do when a man approaches you:

Most likely he's going to say, "What are you reading?" or "Why are you reading in a bar?" Then you close your book and you say, "Why don't you sit down and let's talk about it." Explain why and then follow up on your conversational skills. After you've made contact and talked to him for a while, invite him to meet you somewhere to have a cup of coffee the following day.

If for some reason you get interrupted before you can ask him out, I would suggest saying, "Don, this is very interesting, please call me tomorrow and we will discuss this further." Then give him a business card or personal card with your phone number on it. As a suggestion, you can use a folded business card and on the inside it reads, "I like you very much and I want to see you again! Please call me!

In the beginning you may find it difficult concentrating on reading with all the noise and commotion. With practice you can learn to block out the background noise. You will be interrupted frequently by people's curiosity but that's the main objective.
So why not give it a try. I guarantee you that It works like crazy!

The Card Method

How many times have you been attracted to men, let's say in public places such as a sales clerk, a handsome man alone in a restaurant, a hot & sexy man getting off an airplane alone, or a gorgeous guy standing in the checkout line?

Well I have come up with a get acquainted card for those occasions where you don't have much time or the place is not appropriate for getting acquainted. This card breaks the ice and works like a charm. I've used it and my female friends have used it very successfully to meet men.

Here's what it says and you just take this to your printer and have it printed on a business card and on the back have your name and phone number or email printed. Also you can print your own business cards with the card stock you can buy at Office Depot. It reads:

I've been carrying this card for a long time hoping to meet someone like you. Bars & pickup lines are just not my style, so I hope to meet you using this card. I'd really like to find out who you are and tell you exactly what it was about you that attracted me. My name & phone number or email are on the back of this card. The option of calling or emailing will be yours, but I'll really be sorry if you don't call. Let's spend some time together. Please call or email me and let me know who you are.

Million Dollar Bill Method

This is one of the biggest breakthroughs I've ever seen for meeting new men. What is it? Well, it's a million dollar bill. It looks like the real thing and it's perfectly legal.

Is there such a thing as a real million dollar bill? No, but I swear it looks so real, people will be fooled.

So what does a million dollar bill have to do with meeting men? Well, here are just a few ideas to use the million dollar bill on men:

1. See a man you're attracted to - approach him and say, "You look like a million dollars. Here, have a million dollars on me" and hand him the bill.
2. Proposition men with, "I'll give you this million dollar bill if you will have lunch with me."
3. If you're attracted to the hot waiter that serves your table, do this: Leave a tip with a million dollar and a note that says, "Thanks a million for the great service - Let's get together for lunch. Call me at_____.
3. Do you go to male strip clubs? The million dollar bills are a big hit with the male dancers. Use them to put in his G-string, for conversation pieces, to tip him for a table dance, etc.
4. I'm sure you can think of many other ways to use these million dollar bills to meet men. Try this new way of meeting men. It works!!!

To get your million dollar bills just go to Amazon.com and type in Green Mountain Direct in the search box.

P.S. We are not associated with this company and make no profits off the million dollar bills. We are just passing along this fantastic new way to meet men.

Chapter 8 - How to Talk to a Man

Now I will teach you the art of conversation after you have made contact with a man. Let me tell you what not to do first. Don't make the mistake of coming on with a lot of B.S. about yourself. Don't try to make a big impression by bragging about yourself or your material possessions. The trick to the whole art of conversation is becoming interested in him rather than trying to get him interested in you.

People aren't interested in you. They are interested in themselves - morning, noon, and night. This is an important fact to remember. After all, why should he be interested in you unless you are interested in him first?

It is very important that when you're talking to a man that you face him and look him squarely in the eyes. When talking or listening to him, don't look off to the side or at the ground. Maintain constant eye contact. This gives him a feeling that you care about what he has to say.

During your conversation encourage him to talk about himself, his career, and accomplishments in life. Find out the things he's really into such as sports, politics, cooking, hobbies, art, music, etc. and really zero in on these subjects. This will make him feel closer to you while he's pouring his heart out about his favorite subjects. Just concentrate on talking about him and forget about yourself. While he's talking, acknowledge him with statements like, "Oh yea", "Is that so?", "Wow", and "You're kidding." Also, while talking to him, wear a pleasant smile on your face.

To sum it up, the secret to getting a man to fall in love with you is to talk to a man about himself. Try it and see how he will rattle on and on talking about himself.

Now I will cover some more very important areas of conversation.

Try and spice up your conversation a little bit with things of a sexual nature. After all, most men are just as obsessed with sex as we women may be. Don't be afraid to tell him he has nice muscles, nice legs, awesome biceps. Men don't wear tight-fitting clothes just for the hell of it. They are doing it to turn you on. They want you to become intimate with them.

Remember to be nice in your conversation. Don't say anything mean or try to cut him down. Nice women will finish first when it comes to meeting men. Be warm, charming, and pleasant.

Also, all during your conversation call him by his name as much as possible. His name is music to his ears and to him it's the sweetest and most important sound in any language. This will make him like you. Now, don't forget to say his name often!

Let me tell you about the aggressive conversational approach that doesn't work. Initially, after just meeting him, you ask him to go to bed with you. I just can't understand why some women will rush, push, and expect sexual favors too soon based on some inflated image of their own femininity or what "real" conversation is all about. All they can think about is GET LAID NOW! Coming on too strong after just meeting scares the hell out of some men, especially if he is the shy type.

One of the most common complaints I hear from women at nightclubs is that men want to go to bed right away. They complain that the men have their brains between their legs. Sex is a private and delicate event for many women.

Expecting sex immediately after just meeting puts unnecessary pressure on you. It pays in the long run not to rush or expect sex too quickly or easily.

Of course, there are men out there who will go to bed with you at the drop of a hat, but with the threat of aids and other diseases, a lot of women are particular with who they go to bed with.

So take your time and offer sex with gentleness and quietness. Don't force or demand sex. Let it happen naturally, with the two of you exchanging willing bodies.Also, remember that you should refrain from sex until marriage.

If possible, use your hands, and particularly the tips of your fingers, when talking to a man. The light touch of your fingertips transmits electrifying signals to the other person which will support your thought messages with physical touch.

When touching him while you're talking, be sure it's in a subtle way. Don't do it in a way that would indicate a sexual advance because it may work against you. Just do it casually, like a touch over his hand or on his knee? He will notice these little gestures and slight touches and this will make him feel closer to you.

Finally, your voice is very important when talking to a man. Don't talk in a boring monotone voice. Put emotional emphasis on each and every word you say. Be sure and speak up and don't mutter your words quietly.

Chapter 9 - Body Language

You can attract more men than you can handle just by simply using the art of body language.

How to Use Body Language to Attract Men

Step by step I will guide you in the usage of successful body language using the following methods:

1. Develop a graceful, arrogant sort of walk. A walk that is free and easy with fluid movements. This kind of walk transmits a sexual message which will turn a man's head.

2. When leaning against a wall or whatever, thrust your hips forward, with your legs apart. This position also transmits a sexual message.

3. While you are standing or especially when leaning and you are wearing pants or jeans, hook your thumbs in your belt just above your crotch. Because of your fingers pointing toward your crotch area, this sends out a sexual message to a man and you will be amazed at how many men pick up this signal.

4. Also, while talking to him, wet your lips with your tongue. By using these two techniques, he usually will feel rather excited, and in control.

In conclusion, try these methods of attracting attention from men and see if they work for you. They have worked successfully for a lot of women I know.

Remember, the more techniques you use to attract a man the more men you're going to be meeting and that's the name of the game.

By being able to determine that a man is available in advance, your success ratio in making contact with a man will improve and you will move right in for the kill when you see these signals.

How to Recognize Male Body Language That Means He's Interested In You

The Following body signals and bodily movements will indicate that a man is interested in you after meeting you:

1. Of course, if you do make eye contact and exchange smiles this usually means that he is interested in you.
2. He sits uncomfortably close to you.
3. His hand or thigh carelessly brushes up against your thigh.
4. A man exposes his wrist or palm to you.
5. While talking to you, he twiddles his hair, rearranges his clothes, or pushes his hair away from her face.
6. While talking to you he strokes his wrists or palm.
7. While talking to you he blinks more than usual, fluttering his eyelashes.

8. While talking to you his eyes are brighter than normal. He maintains eye contact and his pupils get bigger.
9. He sits with his legs crossed and pointed towards you.
10. He sits in a very straight position, displaying poise and good posture.
11. While conversing with you he licks his lips.
12. Eyebrows raised and then lowered, then a smile, usually indicates interest.
13. In a crowd he speaks only to you and focuses all of his undivided attention on you.
14. He touches your arm, shoulder, thigh, or hand while talking to you.
15. While conversing with you, he rests an elbow in the palm of one hand, while holding out his other hand, palm up.
16. He raises or lowers the volume of his voice to match yours.
17. He rubs his chin or touches his cheek. This indicates that he's thinking about you and him relating in some way.
18. His skin tone becomes red while being around you.

In conclusion, look for all of these body signals and bodily movements. They sure can be very helpful in evaluating how he feels about you. If you see he's really interested in you, really turn on the charm and give it your best efforts to make a "love connection."

How to Recognize Negative Male Body Language

As you probably know, when someone is sitting or standing with their arms crossed across their chest, it usually means a person does not want to be approached and probably doesn't care to listen to what you have to say. This is how most psychologists interpret the crossed arms.

Don't let this mislead you though. When you see a man with his arms crossed he just may be frustrated and lonely and just not having a good time. However, if he has a stiff and tense look on his face and he is sitting in a stiff manner with his legs tightly crossed and purposely averts his eyes when you try to catch them with your own eyes, you're probably better off not even trying to meet this guy.

A limp or hanging hand usually means he is bored, restless, or just tired. It can also indicate frustration or disgust.

For various reasons, some men do not want to be noticed. They may feel unattractive or even ugly or may not be dressed properly, lack self-confidence, and may feel inferior. They will just stand around shyly or bashfully on the sidelines staring at the ground or watching everyone else have fun. These men may have such a bad complex that they purposely do whatever they can to make themselves less noticeable, such as dressing plainly and wearing a non-becoming hairstyle. In essence these men are saying, "Just leave me alone, and find someone else to talk to."

The really sad part about men like this is that some of them are really attractive. They just have a complex they can't get rid of. If you want to invest a little time you could help them get over this complex. It might be worth the effort.

Chapter 10 - Looks

Do you need to be slender with big boobs to attract and meet men? The answer may surprise you but it's a definite no. With a woman, a man's looks are of critical importance. Not so with a man because they are much more interested in what you're like on the inside than on the outside (well at least they should be). Your personality and warmth of character are of paramount importance to them.

Some men even prefer a woman who is not very attractive, as they usually have a better personality and are more interesting. Just like a lot of handsome men, a real good-looking woman may just sit back passively depending on her looks and are so hung up on themselves they haven't even developed a personality. They're just plain boring and unexciting.

If you do happen to be good-looking, it will be to your advantage though. Good looks and a good body do attract a man's attention.

Your hair is very important to your looks. Most men like a woman with well-groomed hair. I wouldn't advise you to wear your hair real short either. I don't think this is fair, but men like women with long hair. Seek professional help to determine which hairstyle is becoming to you. Try a perm if you like. It can attract men like crazy, especially if it's thick and full. So, be daring and get a perm and see if you don't get more looks from men.

A word about jewelry. Jewelry is in, so wear attractive jewelry to make yourself more becoming and attractive.

A word about watches. Invest some money in an attractive watch. It makes a bad impression when you wear a cheap and ugly watch.

If you really want to turn a man off, go out in public with your hair uncombed, stringy, dirty, and wearing wrinkled, dirty clothes. Some women just don't take enough pride in their appearance and think they can meet men looking like a bum. Well it just doesn't work that way because a man likes a woman to be well-groomed. In public there is certainly no place for a shoddy-looking woman.

If you happen to be obese, resolve here and now that you're going to get rid of all those ugly pounds. With the proper diet and exercise, you can trim yourself down to where you won't be embarrassingly fat.

It's a known fact that if you're a fat slob, your chances of meeting men may be pretty slim. Obesity turns most men off. This doesn't have anything to do with looks but it's worth mentioning. Be sure to take a shower or bath regularly.

Chapter 11 - For Shy Women Only

What is shyness? Webster defines shyness as being "uncomfortable in the presence of others." For the shy woman this refers to being uncomfortable in the presence of the opposite sex.

Shyness can be a crippling mental handicap and its consequences can be devastating in the following ways:

1. Shyness breeds negative feelings like anxiety, depression, and loneliness.
2. It encourages you to think too much about yourself and to be over-preoccupied with your own reactions.
3. It will limit you in voicing your own opinions and values and speaking up for yourself.
4. Shyness hinders your thinking and ability to communicate effectively.
5. It has an unfavorable bearing on how others will evaluate your personality.
6. Shyness makes it more difficult for you to meet new people, make friends, or enjoy potentially good times. Thank goodness, shyness can be cured and overcome!

As an example of shyness, at every nightclub you will find the shy woman. You'll see her just standing around all night, being afraid to approach a man and start up a conversation or even to ask a man to dance. So what happens? They get frustrated and leave the club. They keep coming to the nightclubs and repeat the same routine. They stand around wishing they could meet someone, get frustrated, and then go home frustrated and depressed.

You can overcome your shyness and you "must" if you're going to nightclubs, etc. This kind of social setting can be most threatening and anxiety-provoking if you are a shy woman. This kind of setting will only aggravate your shyness condition if you don't take the appropriate steps to overcome your shyness.

In order for you to promote this change yourself, first you must believe that change is possible. You must really want to overcome your shyness condition. Last, you must be willing to commit time and energy to take action and to risk some temporary failures in initiating change procedures that can lead to long-term success. To sum it up you can change if you believe you can but it takes work...hard work.

Misconceived Beliefs of Shy Women

If I Ask a Man to Dance and He Turns Me Down or If I Talk to a Man and He Ignores Me, It's Because I'm Not Worthwhile or Good Enough For Him.

This irrational belief causes shy women to fear approaching a man and produces low self-esteem when they are rejected. This fear of being rejected and turned down prevents shy women from making contact with men.

If you're turned down for a dance, it doesn't mean that you're not worthwhile or not good enough for him. He just may not feel like dancing at the moment. He may just be tired. He may not even dance. There can be a number of reasons. So don't take it personally. However, what to do in a case like this is to ask him, "Would you like to dance later?" If he says yes, just ask him again later. Even better, just ask him, "Well, can I join you for some conversation?" In the meantime just ask other men to dance. Also, I might add, a lot of women may get turned down to dance, so don't feel that you're the only woman in the world that happens to. It happens to all women, even real good-looking women.

If you approach a man and try to start up a conversation and he ignores you, don't take that personally either. He just may not feel like talking or being bothered. Perhaps he's tied down to a girlfriend or even married. Also, you just might not be using the proper social skills. So if he ignores you, move on to the next man and you'll find someone who will respond to your advances.

The Odds Are Slim of a Man Being Interested and Attracted to Me

This is the woman that has fixed opinions about herself and makes up excuses such as, "I'm not very lucky with men" or "I just don't stand a chance of meeting a man" or "There aren't any good places where I can meet a good man." These are just defensive statements to avoid placing the blame where it really belongs and that's on you. You just haven't tried hard enough to meet a man. That's where the real problem lies.

Make it a point to block these beliefs completely out of your mind because they will hinder you from seeking out men using your own initiative.

If I Stand Around Long Enough Maybe Something Will Happen

Nothing could be farther from the truth. Waiting around for something to happen will most likely accomplish nothing. This will produce little action, if any at all. I just can't tell you how many nights I've wasted at nightclubs just waiting for something to happen, that is until I wised up. If you wait for a man to approach you and strike up a conversation, sometimes you will be waiting all night. You have got to take the initiative and create your own action, it's not going to come to you out of the clear blue sky.

Most Women Are Lucky That Meet and Attract Men

This is a misconceived notion that meeting men happens to other women because of luck and good breaks. Meeting a man rarely happens by accident. Somebody has got to take that first step to initiate contact with a man. The only difference between you and the other woman is she takes action, not because of a stroke of luck. So remember you must go out and initiate action. You must make the effort to meet men.

If a Man Doesn't Show He Likes Me Right Away, He Really Doesn't Like Me and Will Never Like Me

This is an unproductive belief that a man, upon first meeting him, must show complete interest in you by verbal and non-verbal communication.

This is a perfect example of this misconception. You ask a man to dance and he readily accepts. After the dance is over he accepts another woman's invitation to dance. You get all upset and you say to yourself, "If he was really interested in me, he would have found some excuse not to dance with that girl when she asked him."

What this woman doesn't know is that in the majority of cases like this, is when interest is not immediately shown to the other, this doesn't mean that the possibility of liking you may not be there.

So, don't give up on a man if he accepts another girl's invitation to dance. Just keep on pursuing him.

In conclusion, a lot of times a man will not show interest in you following a brief initial meeting. Prolonged communication and conversation are necessary before he can feel comfortable in showing his interest in you.

If You're Really Going to Make It With a Man, You'll Both Know It When You Meet and There Won't Be Any Problems

This is the woman who is waiting for "love at first sight" to occur to initiate a relationship. Upon meeting a man, if there are no vibrations or chemistry between them she simply dismisses the encounter. She uses this as a defensive excuse for initiating any intimate contact with men.

Waiting for "love at first sight" will prevent you from establishing real friendships with the opposite sex out of casual acquaintances. You don't have to be madly in love with a man to show interest and to establish a friendly rapport.

How to Overcome Shyness at Nightclubs

The following is a guide to use in overcoming your shyness at nightclubs. Follow these steps and you can overcome your shyness and start meeting men instead of standing on the sidelines watching other women meet men at nightclubs.

1. One of the biggest roadblocks to a shy woman meeting men is fear. Fear that she will be rejected, fear that she won't know what to say, and fear that she won't know how to act.

Believe me, there is nothing to fear but fear it. Fear and anxiety will produce distinct psychological consequences and if there's anything that's going to hinder your success in meeting men, it is going to be fear.

The fear of being rejected by a man can paralyze your attempts to meet men. Accept the fact that you're going to get rejected some of the time. Just because you get rejected by a man it does not make you worthless. There can be many different reasons why a man may not be interested in you at a given moment. Most of these reasons have little or nothing to do with you as a person. Being rejected by a man is just a risk you will have to take and if you 'd get rejected by a man, it's certainly not the end of the world.

Keep this in mind if you get rejected by a man at a nightclub. No matter how many men are not interested in you, you must remember there are many other men at the nightclub, many of whom would be delighted to know you.

To overcome these fears and meet men, you have got to approach it like you would if you were going to jump in a cold ocean to go swimming. Hurl yourself into it. TAKE ACTION! This is a really good cure!

You have got to practice meeting men. Sure, you'll get rejected a few times. We all do. So what if you get rejected. You may never see him again anyway. By practicing, you'll build up your confidence. Also, by accepting the fact that you're only practicing meeting men, the pressure to succeed won't be so great.

2. Has this ever happened to you? You see this really handsome guy that you would love to approach. You try to build up your nerve but you make excuses like, "I'm too scared" or "I'm too nervous."

Pondering, stalling, postponing, reconsidering, these are all delaying tactics that impede action. If you find yourself telling yourself these lies and making excuses, block them out of your mind immediately and take action and approach that man right then and there. Don't waste any time or you'll see one man after another walk right out of your life. Don't delay trying to meet a man or you might find yourself delaying all your life.

3. Get rid of the idea that people are always watching you, sizing you up and evaluating you. The only people that do this are shy people who spend a lot of time fearing that they are being evaluated negatively. The reason you think you are being watched is because you do this to others.

The solution to breaking this habit is to stop judging and sizing people up and you will stop thinking that others are doing the same to you. Don't worry about people evaluating you unfavorably because the reason for this is that they think they are better than you.

4. Shy women have difficulty in carrying on a conversation with the opposite sex. You're going to have to work on sharpening up your conversational skills. If you don't have any skills, you're going to have to develop some. You're not going to meet many men at nightclubs unless you talk to them.

I have given you conversational guidelines to use in Chapter Eight on conversation. Put into practice these guidelines and I promise you that you will develop conversational skills and know how to carry on a conversation with a man.

5. Employ the methods used in Chapter Fourteen on "Meeting Men Using A Hypnotic Sleep Tape." Using these methods will condition your subconscious mind to meet men. Your mind will literally be saturated with meeting and attracting men. This in turn, will help you to overcome your shyness.

6. Use the "mirror technique" described in Chapter Sixteen. The only modification you will need to make on this is what you say in front of the mirror. Tell yourself these commands:

(a) "When I go to a nightclub, I will now feel very relaxed and comfortable around men."
(b) "I now overcome my shyness and meet lots of men at nightclubs."
(c) "When I see a man I'd like to meet, I now approach him immediately instead of making up excuses as to why I shouldn't approach him."
(d) "Now, I'm not standing around all night waiting for something to happen. Now I make something happen. I will take action."
(e) "Now, I don't stand around waiting for a man to approach me. I'm now taking the initiative to make contact."
(f) "If a man rejects me, now I don't let it hurt my feelings."

You can use any or all these positive suggestions or even make up your own.

7. Use the method outlined in Chapter Sixteen on "Meeting Men Using Mental Pictures." On your cards write the word "Confident." When you see this word, picture yourself at nightclubs as a confident woman in control, making contact with men. Picture yourself not being shy with men anymore, but a woman that is confident in her abilities to attract men.

Another good word to use is "Contact." When you look at this word, picture yourself making verbal contact with men at nightclubs. Picture yourself approaching men and talking to them.

8. Use the method outlined in Chapter Fourteen on "Meeting Men Using Autosuggestion." You can use the suggestions given in (6) of this section for your suggestions used for this method.
9. I highly recommend that you read books on shyness. There are many excellent books on the market to help you overcome shyness. In some cities there are shyness clinics you can attend which can be helpful.

10. You can order the shyness tape from POTENTIALS UNLIMITED. By listening to the tape daily for at least 30 days, you will become more confident and will feel an increase of self-esteem. Your fears and shyness will gradually disappear, in most cases.

To order this tape go to: Go to their website at: www.potentialsunlimited.com and order the tape on shyness. More information is listed in Chapter Thirteen.

11. Finally, these steps to overcoming shyness can only help you if you have made the decision to change your life. The most powerful ingredient you possess in overcoming your shyness is the power of your own mind.

The key to making this change in your life is to believe that change is possible. Also, you must really want to change. You must have the willpower to commit time, effort, and energy to overcoming your shyness and to risk some short-term failures.

Chapter 12 - How to Meet Men Using Self-Hypnosis

With the proper understanding and proper application of self-hypnosis, this method of meeting men can be highly successful.

First of all let me explain what self-hypnosis is and what it can do for you. You must understand the relationship between the conscious and the subconscious mind. For the purpose of explanatory purposes consider the mind being made up of two parts, the conscious and the subconscious.

The conscious mind directs all reasoned action and the subconscious mind controls your automatic responses.

The conscious mind has been referred to as the "Mind of Man." With the reasoning power of the mind, man can direct his own destiny if he so desires.

The subconscious mind responds because of conditioned instincts. A good example is when you hear a sudden and loud noise and it makes you jump. This is not through reasoning of the conscious mind but from a conditioned fear in your subconscious mind.

The subconscious mind has no powers of reason, so everything it accepts is perceived as truth. It accepts and acts upon any fact or suggestion given to it by the conscious mind. While in a state of self-hypnosis you will practice picking up and meeting men successfully, even if you're a shy woman. All this will register in your subconscious mind and when it's time for action, your conscious mind will just simply act it out.

With repeated practice of meeting men in your mind while in a state of self-hypnosis, meeting men will become just automatic. You will feel relaxed and natural when around men and not feel nervous and tense when approaching them. Everything you do will have already been practiced over and over in your subconscious mind.

To avoid any confusion, let me explain that you will not be meeting men while in a hypnotic state. You will simply be in a light hypnotic state while in the privacy of your home while practicing self-hypnosis. During actual practice of meeting men you will only trigger your subconscious mind to act out the things that you have fed it to do. This is a natural process and as normal as walking. It's not harmful and every day you practice the use of the subconscious mind in your daily activities.

There are many good books on how and why self-hypnosis works, so I won't go into great detail on these areas. The main thing I want to do is teach you how to use self hypnosis to meet men anywhere.

How to Achieve a State of Self-Hypnosis

Now, we will learn how to achieve a state of self-hypnosis. First of all and most important of all, you must believe that self-hypnosis works, is safe, and have no fears about it.

Choose a room that is quiet and dimly lit. Make sure that you will be undisturbed because you need total quietness and concentration. You may choose to sit in a comfortable chair or lay in your bed. What I personally feel is more relaxing, is lying in the bed. The most effective method is inducing self-hypnosis upon retiring for the night.

Have no fears about inducing self-hypnosis because you're not going to do anything you don't want to do and you won't stay in a hypnotic state if you desire to come out of it.

The directions that you give to yourself don't have to be spoken out loud. You can give your commands silently in your mind.

The following is an example of a method to induce self-hypnosis:

Before retiring at night, turn the lights out and lie down in your bed and find a comfortable position. Close your eyes and repeat the following to yourself:

I am now going to relax every single muscle in my body, starting with from my toes to my head. Start with the right leg first, from the toes to the hip. My right toes are very relaxed...They feel very heavy and limp...This feeling is now spreading to my right ankle...Now my right foot is totally relaxed and limp...Repeat the same procedure for the left foot...Now both feet are totally relaxed...Heavy and limp...This feeling is now spreading to my right calf...My right leg is totally relaxed from my toes to my knee...This feeling is now spreading to my left calf and relaxing my left leg from the toes to the knee...Both my legs are totally relaxed and limp from the toes to the knee...This relaxed feeling is now spreading to my right thigh...Now my right leg is totally relaxed from the tip of my toes to my hip...Now I'm relaxing my left thigh too...So both my legs are relaxed and limp...Heavy and relaxed...So relaxed...So limp...Now I feel my right hand getting heavy....So relaxed and so limp....The fingers are getting very heavy...Limp...So relaxed...My right hand is now totally relaxed and heavy...This relaxed feeling is now flowing up my right arm to my shoulder...Now I feel my left hand getting heavy...So relaxed and so limp...The fingers are now getting heavy...Limp...So relaxed...My left hand is now totally relaxed and heavy...This relaxed feeling is now flowing up my left arm to my shoulder...Both of my arms and hands are now completely relaxed...So very limp...So heavy...I am now going to relax my body...My hips...My back muscles...My stomach...My chest muscles...My shoulders...They will relax all at the same time...Now I will take a deep breath and hold it...I will release it very slowly...My entire body is now relaxing...I am taking a deep breath, slowly...My body is totally relaxed now...I feel so relaxed and limp...I am now breathing slowly and evenly...My neck is now feeling very relaxed and limp...My head is becoming so heavy...So very heavy...The muscles in my face are growing limp and relaxed...From my neck to the top of my head is completely relaxed...My body is totally relaxed...And so heavy...So relaxed...Every muscle and every nerve in my entire body is completely at ease.

The preceding procedure doesn't have to be done word for word. The idea is to relax your body one part at a time until your entire body is relaxed.

After giving instructions to each part of your body to relax, be sure and pause until you feel it working. Be sure and don't will your body to relax. Your conscious mind comes into play when you will your body and this defeats your purpose.

When you have now reached the state of total relaxation over your entire body, open your eyes. Pick out an object above eye level. A good focal point would be where the wall joins the ceiling, a light reflection, a picture frame, etc. At this moment you will try to get your eyelids to close involuntarily on a specific count. You can use the count of three, ten, or whatever numbers you so desire. If upon completion of your count, you have an uncontrollable urge to close your eyes, you are in a state of self-hypnosis. This is the very first test in determining whether you have reached a state of self-hypnosis. When counting, go very slowly. If your eyes do not close upon completion of the count, start over again. They may close the first time you try it and then again it may take you anywhere from five to fifteen minutes. With practice every night, the time required for eye closure will decrease.

Let's say you attempt to get an eye closure but the test fails to work. The reasons you don't get an eye closure are usually the following:

1. You are not taking enough time to relax. Being in a totally relaxed state of mind is very critical.
2. You are not in the right psychological state of mind. Perhaps you are worried about something or your mind is cluttered with emotional turmoil.
3. Your conditioning process has not been sufficiently established.

If you are beset by any of these problems, just take more time to enter a good state of relaxation and tell yourself you are going to be in a very beneficial and pleasurable state of mind.

If all else fails, and this is very important, if you can't get eye closure voluntarily, then close them voluntarily and go ahead with the desired post hypnotic suggestions as though you were actually in the hypnotic state.

Here are some suggestions as to how to achieve the eye closure test:

When I complete the count of ten my eyelids will become very tired, heavy, and watery. Even before the count of ten is completed it may become necessary to close my eyelids. When I do, I will fall into a deep state of self-hypnosis. I will be totally conscious, be able to hear everything, and be able to give my subconscious mind suggestions. The following doesn't have to be repeated word for word, just the form is important.

One...My eyelids are becoming very heavy...Oh so very heavy...Two...My eyelids are growing very tired and weary...Oh so very tired and weary...Three...My eyelids are becoming very watery...Oh so watery...Oh so watery...Four...I can just barely keep my eyes open...Five...My eyes are beginning to close...Six... My eyelids are beginning to close more and more...Seven...My mind and body are completely relaxed and totally at ease...Eight...It is now becoming just impossible to keep my eyelids open...Nine...It is now impossible to keep my eyelids open...Ten...My eyes are now closed and I am in a state of self-hypnosis and I can give myself the post-hypnotic suggestions I desire.

Now using the following example, you will mentally picture yourself meeting men at nightclubs (this does not have to be nightclubs, it can be anywhere). Picture in your mind and tell yourself the following suggestions after you have reached a state of self-hypnosis and achieved eye-closure.

1. Before you leave, you look in the mirror and see a very attractive, sexy, and charming woman. You have a very charming smile on your face and a sexy gleam in your eyes that can literally melt a man.
2. I'm going to meet a special man tonight and have the time of my life.
3. You walk in the nightclub and see all these hot and sexy men just dying to meet you.
4. You start walking around to check out the action. As you're walking, several men notice you and your eyes meet.
5. You see a handsome man who catches your eye and you approach him.
6. You ask him to dance and while you're dancing you look into each other's eyes and there's a powerful magnetic attraction between you.
7. You introduce yourself while dancing and ask him what his name is.
8. When you're through dancing you ask him if you can join him for a drink. He says, "Yes."
9. You join him at his table or stand with him if he has no table.
10. You start conversing with him about himself and you start hitting it off really well together mentally.
11. A slow song comes on and you ask him to dance.

12. While slow-dancing, you hold him close and your crotches are rubbing against each other. A heat of passion begins to build. He kisses you on the neck and then on the lips.

13. The song is over and the mission is accomplished. You have made initial physical contact and it will be smooth sailing the rest of the night.

14. Well, it's getting close to closing time and you ask him if he would like to come over to your place for a drink. He accepts your invitation.

15. After you get to your apartment, you fix him a drink, turn the lights down low, and put on some soft music.

16. You start kissing and caressing him and one thing leads to another and both of you end up making mad passionate love to each other.

Finally, just let your imagination run wild and visualize anything you want happening to you at the nightclub. This is just an example. You can visualize yourself meeting men anywhere you choose after you've reached a state of self-hypnosis.

In conclusion, these suggestions should be carefully thought out and planned beforehand so you will know what to tell your subconscious mind.

Post Hypnotic Suggestions

After you have completed these suggestions for meeting men in your subconscious mind, give yourself post-hypnotic suggestions that the next time you induce self-hypnosis you will enter a deeper state more quickly. Using this technique, say to yourself:

The next time I practice self-hypnosis...I will fall into a deeper and more relaxed state of mind...Relaxing my body will come more quickly...And more easily...The next time I go to_____(name of place), my mind and body will be totally relaxed and self-confident...My mind will be at ease...The mental pictures and suggestions I have just experienced ...Will come into play...And meeting men will be as easy as pie...I know these positive suggestions and mental pictures will work for me...At the count of three...I will open my eyes...I will feel completely relaxed...At the count of count of three...I will feel totally refreshed...I will feel wide awake and alert...I will feel a renewed source of energy.

Alternate Method

The following is another method of achieving a state of self-hypnosis, along with suggestions for the subconscious mind.

Procedure #1

Choose a quiet room where you will be undisturbed. This room should be dimly lit, but enough light for you to read by. The room should have a peaceful and comfortable atmosphere.

Now, relax in your favorite easy-chair or lay down on your bed. Do not lay completely flat. Your body should be flat with your feet elevated, but your head and shoulders should be propped up with a pillow. Get as comfortable as possible and close your eyes. Relax every muscle in your body.

Now clear your mind of all thoughts. Simply relax...and think of nothing. Think of absolutely nothing. Block out all noises and distractions. Keep your eyes closed.

Procedure #2

You will silently command each individual part of your body to relax (actually feel each body-part totally relax as you give each command).

1. Command your feet to relax (take your time and actually FEEL them relaxing).
2. Command your ankles to relax.
3. Command your calves to relax (feel the muscles in your calves relaxing).
4. Command your knees to relax.

5. Command your thighs to relax (feel every muscle in your thighs relaxing).
NOTE: (Don't rush. Take your time between each and every command).
6. Command your stomach to relax (feel your stomach muscles relaxing).
7. Command your chest muscles to relax (feel them relaxing).
8. Command your shoulders to relax (feel them relaxing).
9. Command your upper arms to relax.
10. Command your elbows to relax.
11. Command your forearms to relax.
12. Command your wrists to relax.
13. Command your hands to relax (feel each finger and joint in your hands relaxing).
14. Command your lower back to relax.
15. Command your upper back to relax (feel all the muscles in your upper and lower back relaxing).
16. Command all the muscles in the back of your neck to relax (feel them relaxing).
17. Command the back of your head and scalp to relax.
18. Command all the muscles in your face to relax (feel your eyes, mouth, cheeks, etc. relaxing).
19. Command your entire body to relax (actually feel all your muscles, joints, nerves and mind totally relaxed).

At this point, your whole body should be completely relaxed. Your mind should also be relaxed and free of all thought. You should be thinking of nothing.

Procedure #3

Now you will relax your mind and body even more now.

With your eyes still closed...with your mind blank...and with every muscle in your body totally relaxed, begin to count from 1 to 20 slowly.

As you count, tell yourself that your mind and body are becoming more and more relaxed.

As you count 1-2-3-4, feel your mind and body becoming more relaxed.

As you count from 5 to 16, feel yourself going into a deeper and deeper state of relaxation.

As you count 17-18-19 and finally 20, tell yourself (and actually FEEL) that you are now in a very relaxed, almost sleep-like condition - with your mind and body totally relaxed and your mind completely free of all worry, problems, emotions, etc. Think of nothing!

You are now ready to give your subconscious mind suggestions. You must say these suggestions to yourself with "feeling" and "emotion." You must believe and have faith and confidence that these principles will work for you. This is very important to your success with self-hypnosis! You must "see", "feel", and "believe" each suggestion.

Putting Self-Hypnosis Into Action

After completing procedures 1, 2, and 3, open your eyes long enough
to read the following suggestion. Read it to yourself a few times...
"I AM COMPLETELY RELAXED WHENEVER I SPEAK TO MEN"

Now...close your eyes and repeat the suggestion to yourself several more times...WITH BELIEF!

As you say the suggestion to yourself, SEE yourself talking to men. FEEL yourself being totally relaxed while talking to them. BELIEVE that you actually are completely relaxed as you talk to men.

Procedure #4

Open your eyes just long enough to read the next suggestion. Read it a few times.

"I AM TOTALLY CONFIDENT AND COMPLETELY SELF-ASSURED WHENEVER I SPEAK TO MEN - ESPECIALLY ATTRACTIVE MEN"

Now, close your eyes and repeat the above suggestion to yourself several more times. And...as before...repeat it to yourself with belief.

As you say the above suggestion to yourself, SEE yourself talking to men. SEE yourself talking to handsome men. BELIEVE that you actually do have the confidence and self-assurance necessary to hold a conversation with absolutely any man you choose.

Procedure #5

Go through the remaining suggestions following the same procedure as outlined above.

NOTE: It is very, very important that you use the SEE...FEEL...BELIEVE technique for each suggestion. This is the only way you will be able to reach your subconscious mind, and thus, receive positive results.

NOTE: You are to open your eyes between each suggestion ONLY until they are memorized. Once memorized, simply keep your eyes closed throughout the entire procedure. You should memorize the suggestions as soon as possible...as it will be more beneficial to you to keep your eyes closed throughout the entire procedure.

NOTE: Do not get discouraged if you find it somewhat awkward (at first) when trying to "see", "feel", and "believe" each suggestion. This is to be expected.

You will become more and more at ease with these principles each day you practice them.

You're Remaining Daily Suggestions

* I ALWAYS SAY THE RIGHT THINGS WHENEVER I SPEAK TO MEN. I ALWAYS KNOW EXACTLY WHAT TO SAY.

* I ALWAYS KNOW WHAT NOT TO SAY TO MEN.

* I NEVER HAVE TO ACT "COOL" WITH MEN. I AM COOL ENOUGH THE WAY I AM. MEN NOTICE THIS QUALITY IN ME AND LIKE ME FOR BEING ME.

* IT IS EXTREMELY EASY FOR ME TO WALK UP TO ANY MAN AND START TALKING TO HIM.

* WHEN I SEE A MAN I LIKE, I AM ABLE TO MOVE INTO ACTION QUICKLY AND EASILY.

* I REALIZE THAT SOME MEN SIMPLY ARE NOT INTER-ESTED IN WOMEN...SO IF I GET TURNED DOWN BY A MAN, I QUICKLY FORGET ABOUT IT AND MOVE ON TO ANOTHER MAN.

* EACH TIME I TRY TO MEET A MAN IS EASIER THAN THE TIME BEFORE.

* WHENEVER I APPROACH A MAN, I AM TOTALLY FREE FROM ALL NEGATIVE FEELINGS...SUCH AS WORRY, INFERIORITY OR NERVOUSNESS.

* I ALWAYS THINK IN TERMS OF SUCCEEDING WHENEVER I APPROACH A MAN. I NEVER THINK IN TERMS OF FAILURE.

* I ALWAYS EXPECT MEN TO SAY "YES" WHENEVER I SUGGEST WE GET TOGETHER SOMETIME.

* I REALIZE THAT MOST MEN I MEET ARE QUIET ANXIOUS TO HAVE ME ASK THEM FOR A DATE. KNOWING THIS, I AM COMPLETELY RELAXED AND SELF-CONFIDENT WHENEVER I ASK A MAN FOR A DATE.

* MY FAILURE DAYS WITH MEN ARE GONE FOREVER. I AM A NEW WOMAN AND SEE MYSELF THROUGH THE "SUCCESS" EYE OF NOW.

* I PUSH DEFEAT INTO MY PAST...AND LOOK BEYOND IT FOR SUCCESS.

* I CLOSE THE DOOR TIGHTLY ON MY PAST BAD EXPERIENCES WITH MEN...AND KEEP IT CLOSED.

* I AM A MATURE PERSON AND SEEK EVEN GREATER GROWTH WITHIN MYSELF.

* AS FAR AS MEETING, DATING, AND SEDUCING MEN IS CONCERNED, I HAVE ABSOLUTELY NO LIMITATIONS.

* I AM SUCCESSFUL IN ALL MY RELATIONS WITH MEN.

Procedure #6

After completing your daily suggestions, remain relaxed. Remain in the same position and relax your whole body. Think of nothing...keep your eyes closed...and just relax...Now just relax...relax...relax...relax and enjoy it...relax...

After two or three minutes of this you will be ready to come out of self-hypnosis.

Coming Out of Self-Hypnosis

With your eyes still closed...and your mind blank...start counting backwards from 20 down to 1. Count slowly.

As you count down...20-19-18-17-16-15...feels your body and mind begin to "awaken." (Your eyes should remain closed).

As you count down...14-13-12-11-10...now, start to become aware of the sounds and atmosphere around you.

As you count down...9-8-7-6...say to yourself: "When I open my eyes, I will feel simply GREAT! I will feel totally rested and greatly refreshed. When I open my eyes, I will feel great. I will be full of energy and will feel greatly refreshed." (All the while you are saying the above, believe it!).

As you count down...5-4-3-2..."Feel" yourself starting to Feel just great. "FEEL" yourself starting to come "alive."

And finally, as you say 1...OPEN YOUR EYES...and immediately GET UP!!!

FINAL NOTE: Each self-hypnosis session should last about twenty minutes. And you should have a session once a day...every day.

Also, do not use these principles very late at night or when you are very tired. By doing so, you may easily fall asleep (something which we do not want to happen).

The best time to practice self-hypnosis is midmorning, mid-afternoon, or evening.

Use either of these self-hypnosis methods or both. They are both equally effective. With practice, you will be amazed at the results. You will be meeting more men and doing it more easily. It will just come naturally to you.

Chapter 13 - How to Meet Men
Using a Hypnotic Sleep CD

Within you is the ability to pick up or meet any man you desire. It is only awaiting the stimulation of your desire to spring forth and bring you whatever man you want.

You have the key to that door. Only you can unlock it. ONLY YOU. And for you a hypnotic sleep CD can be the first step in unlocking that door.

Potentials Unlimited of Bradenton, FL offers a self-hypnosis CD containing complete instructions on how to give yourself suggestions, along with detailed procedures for entering a state of self-hypnosis.

Using it, you will be guided into a state of hypnosis with key phrases and statements so you can utilize this level of mind anytime you choose. When you have reached a good depth, there's a quiet space on the tape where you can enter your own suggestions into your subconscious mind. Then, after a bit, you're guided back to awakening consciousness.

At the end of this chapter I will tell you which suggestions to enter in the quiet space on the tape and how to order this CD.

How Hypnotic Sleep Cd's Work

Each of these professionally produced cds is designed to bypass your conscious mind. It is this, the subconscious that is the real power center of your being. The subconscious mind is the seat of memory, the monitor of all bodily processes. It regulates your heart, plays chemist for your digestive system, and analyzes input from your senses like an ultra-sophisticated computer (which it is). Your subconscious is a magical property, existing deep within you.

Your subconscious will accept, and then bring into reality, any suggestion presented to it. When the suggestions are positive, dominant, and accompanied with visual imagery, as in hypnosis, the results are amazing.

How Hypnotic Sleep Cd's Are Used at Bedtime

Using a hypnotic sleep CD, a series of suggestions are first given to your conscious mind to bring about a pleasant state of relaxation.

If the CD is played at your sleep time, you will probably drift off into a natural sleep. This is highly desirable because the subconscious mind never sleeps, and will accept suggestions far better without my interference from your conscious mind.

Repeated playing of the CD at bedtime will completely saturate the subconscious mind with positive suggestions, designed to bring about positive changes within you.

How Hypnotic Sleep CD'S Are Used During the Day

Your conscious mind will not be fully aware of the suggestions given to your subconscious. Therefore, playing the CD several times a week in a relaxing and restful position will be necessary.

Listening to the CD during the day will allow you to experience the pleasant sensations of light hypnosis. You will find yourself floating smoothly into a dreamlike state of mind, much like twilight sleep or daydreaming.

During this daytime playing, your conscious mind will become saturated with the same messages your subconscious mind has been absorbing during the evening.

How It All Works Together For You

By using the CD at two different times, your conscious and subconscious mind will begin to work in harmony. The results are dramatic. Positive changes you've desired happen and you meet men as if by magic.

It's your mind and it's programming that makes up your world.

Look around at your world. What would you like to change, eliminate, to improve, to make better for yourself?

Hypnosis is a very effective tool for change. Hypnotic sleep cd's are simple, easy, inexpensive ways to achieve this change. In fact, they could be the most important thing you've ever done for your life, not to mention your love-life.

How to Use Your Sleep CD to Meet Men

Go to their website at: www.potentialsunlimited.com

Order their CD titled, "SELF HYPNOSIS MS." Using this CD you will be put into a state of self-hypnosis with key phrases and statements so you can put into use this level of mind anytime you desire. There's a quiet space on the CD where you can enter your own suggestions into your mind. This title is also available in MP3 format.

Now I will give you an example of the suggestions to use.

You don't have to use these suggestions word for word. You can make up your own suggestions for any type of circumstance or situation for meeting men. Here's a sample recording:

As I'm getting ready to go to the nightclub tonight, I look into the mirror and see this attractive and sexy woman, a woman with a very sexy look about her with a charming smile that can literally melt a man...Before I leave I am thoroughly convinced in my mind that I will meet a special man at the nightclub...Upon arriving at the nightclub I will feel very confident and totally relaxed...As I walk through the nightclub to check out the action, I catch the eyes of several attractive men...They're all giving me that, "I'd love to meet you" look...There's so many eligible men to choose from it's unbelievable...I can have any man I desire...While cruising the nightclub I see this very attractive man and our eyes meet...The magnetism between us is overpowering...I approach him and say, "Hi, would you like to dance?"...He says, "Yes, I'd love to"...We get out on the dance floor and start dancing to the pulsating beat...Watching the way he moves his hips and crotch are driving me out of my mind...Our eyes meet and we both smile...I can tell by the way he looks at me that he's interested in me...I ask him, "What's your name?"...Then he tells me his name...The song ends and we're having such a good time we keep on dancing on and on...We mutually agree to take a break and I say, "Can I join you for some conversation?"...He replies, "Sure"...I join him at his table and begin getting him to talk about himself...By this time we're really hitting it off really good conversationally...After making this initial contact, I ask him to dance again...We dance several songs again and we both feel drawn to each other like magnets...Finally a slow song comes on...Now is my chance to make some real physical contact...As we dance, our crotches begin to rub...I begin to caress his back with my hands and he does the same to me...I begin kissing his neck and working my way up to his ear lobe...He's becoming just as excited as I am and begins kissing me very gently and softly on my neck...Now our lips meet and the vibrations are so strong we can hardly keep our balance while dancing...I'm having the time of my life tonight and I feel so good...The song ends and we return to our table...It's getting kind of late now...I ask him if he would like to leave and get something to eat...He accepts the invitation and we go to a restaurant...After we finish our food, I ask him if he would like to come over for a drink...He accepts and before you know it we are at my apartment...I fix him a drink and put some soft music on and turn the lights down low...We both are feeling so relaxed and comfortable...Our lips meet and the passion begins building up...He is responding to all of my physical advances...Now we are making mad passionate love to each other...He spends the night and before he goes home I get his phone number for future reference...My head is up in the clouds and I keep saying to myself, "It's so easy meeting men at nightclubs"...I'm going back again and I will make a "love connection" again...This I'm sure of...And sure enough, I go back and the same things happen all over again...This is really exciting meeting so many different men and being so successful at it...I can attract any man I desire...I'm the envy of all the women that just stand around on the sidelines...They're amazed at my ability to meet men...I am totally confident in my abilities and skill in meeting men at nightclubs or anywhere.

Using this CD can do wonders for your love life. Just listen to it before you retire at night and once during the day while you are awake. You should listen to this tape for at least 30 days to get the full benefit from it.

Chapter 14 - How to Meet Men Using Autosuggestion

This will help you to meet men by influencing the subconscious mind by means of suggestion. Using the method of autosuggestion, you will be giving yourself positive suggestions to meet men.

This method is very simple and very effective. Repetition is the main rule in making suggestions work. They should be repeated three or four times, or even more. These suggestions can be made verbally, though it is not necessary to say the words aloud. Just thinking about them is enough. Some people respond better if they are said aloud, so you might want to experiment to see what works best for you. To make the suggestion more potent, you may form a visual image while making the suggestion verbally. There is a tendency for the subconscious to carry out any prolonged and repeated visual image.

You will be phrasing your suggestions using the words, "I can" or "I will." Start out using the words, "I can" and if no results are shown, switch over to the words, "I will." Remember, in giving yourself suggestions, acceptance by the inner mind is necessary or it will not be carried out, no matter how badly you may consciously want this.

Now I will recommend these suggestions for you to use. Pick out the ones you like the most or even make up your own. Any of them will work.

"I can walk up to any man and start talking to him."

"I can move into action quickly and easily when I see a man I like."
"I can approach a man, totally free from all negative feelings such as worry, inferiority or nervousness."
"I can bring a man home with me if I choose to do so, when I go to nightclubs."
"I can meet any man I desire."

It is recommended that you shouldn't burden your subconscious mind with too many suggestions at one time. Try to work on one suggestion at a time and never more than two. If using two suggestions, start with the first one and repeat it three or four times, then repeat the second suggestion three or four times, then go back and repeat the first suggestion.

Use this method daily and you will be meeting more men than you ever dreamed possible. You will be more confident than ever and meeting men will become natural and easy. Try this and see if your love-life doesn't improve dramatically.

Also, I might add, you can use this method to obtain anything you want. It doesn't have to be applied to just meeting men only.

In conclusion, remember the need for repetition and suggest results, not means.

Chapter 15 - The Mirror Technique for Meeting and Men

This is a very effective method of releasing the power of the subconscious mind by using a mirror. This method is very effective in motivating you to meet men. It can be used to obtain anything you so desire.

Now I will explain the technique. Stand in front of a mirror. The mirror does not have to be full length, but you should at least be able to see yourself from the waste up.

Stand fully erect just like a soldier does when told to come to attention. Now take three or four deep breaths until you feel a sense of enormous strength, power, and determination. Now look into the very depths of your eyes and tell yourself, "Every time I go to a nightclub I will meet a very special man that I'm attracted to." This is just an example of what to tell yourself and be sure to say this aloud so you can see your lips move and hear the words uttered. Also, you can make up your own words and suggestions or even use the ones in the previous section on autosuggestion.

Do this exercise regularly at least twice a day, in the morning and in the evening and you will be astonished at the results. You may augment this by writing any slogans or key words associated with your desires with soap on the face of your mirror, such as "LOVE CONNECTION", "TAKE ACTION", "SCORE", etc.

Within a few days after practicing this exercise you will really begin to feel a sense of confidence in yourself and your abilities to meet men that you never have felt before.

It is advisable not to tell anyone about your using this method to meet men. There are scoffers and skeptics that may ridicule you and shake your confidence.

Chapter 16 - Meeting Men
Using Mental Pictures

It is a known fact that whatever a man can conceive mentally, he can bring into materialization. Meeting men must follow if the proper mental pictures are created and maintained, for this sets in motion the law of cause and effect.

To help you create the mental pictures of meeting men, I will describe a very effective method to saturate your subconscious mind with mental pictures.

You will need about four cards. The back of business cards will do just great. Just write the word, "LOVE CONNECTION" or any other word you associate with meeting men with on these cards.

Carry one in your purse, place one on your bathroom mirror, place one by your bed, then another one where you work. Whenever you look at these cards, mentally picture yourself meeting men at various places such as nightclubs, the beach, swimming pools, etc. By placing these cards in various areas, this will enable you to see mentally, the pictures at all hours of the day.

In addition to using the cards during the day, it is best to look at them before you go to sleep at night and upon waking in the morning and mentally picture yourself meeting many men. These two periods of the day are highly important moments to concentrate upon thoughts with added force. It is helpful to form these pictures throughout the day because the more often you form your pictures backed with desire, the speedier the materialization.

In conclusion, you should tell nobody what the words on the cards mean or give anyone any suggestion as to what you are trying to accomplish. Just keep it to yourself. Any outside ridicule or criticism can be detrimental to your success with these methods.

Chapter 17 - How to Use Telepathy to Meet Men

Telepathy is the sending and receiving of thought messages without words being spoken. Thoughts pass from your mind to another's mind through a sea of electrons which surround us. Thought is a real thing just like any visible object. Thought sends out vibrations just as light and heat do, but much more intense.

To employ this method, you will simply be looking in the direction of a man and you will be sending forth positive thought images, conveying a message such as, "I would like to meet you." While sending the message you will be looking at him with a steady gaze.

The eye is an important factor in influencing people. It has the power of impressing your will upon another. In using this method, you will need to develop a magnetic gaze. To develop the magnetic gaze, practice the following exercise:

Stand in front of a large mirror with your face about 15 inches from it. You can also use a small mirror placed on a table. Using ink, make a small dot at the base of your nose, squarely between your eyes. Focus your eyes upon the dot, while staring in the mirror, and gaze at it firmly without winking. If you get the urge to wink, just raise your eyelids a little and this should prevent you from winking. Keep practicing this until you can gaze at the mirror without winking for about fifteen seconds.

While using this magnetic gaze, a man will either react positively or he will break the gaze coming from you. If he won't look at you, you'll have to assume perhaps that he might not be interested in you. However, you may want to just try harder. If he responds to your gaze and your silent message, you will soon see the results.

Now, I will describe how to use these telepathic powers.

First of all, don't let your mind wander while you are trying to make contact with a man. Concentrate all your thoughts on the task at hand.

Pick out a man and give him your magnetic gaze. While looking at him, send out a thought such as, "Come over here and talk to me" or "Come home with me." You can make your own messages to send, these are just examples. Just repeat your message over and over in your mind in a relaxed manner and make your message short and to the point.

Don't tell others you are using mental telepathy to influence others. Their skepticism or ridicule may weaken your faith.

Also, you must not use this power to bring harm to others or to send unkind thoughts.

That's all there is to it. Using this method, you can make contact with a man without uttering a single word.

With practice, men will receive your thoughts and act upon them. Just imagine how much fun it will be, controlling the thoughts of men and being able to influence a man with your mind. After you have learned how to use mental telepathy, you will be able to actually will a man to get up and come over and talk to you.

In conclusion, try this method and you will find yourself meeting more men.

Chapter 18 - Goal-Setting

Goal-setting is a powerful system in getting what you want and this is, scoring with hot & sexy men. "As you think, so you become." If you focus on a goal with determination, backed with a burning desire, you'll experience it. Setting a goal to meet men is acknowledging to your conscious and subconscious minds that where you stand as far as scoring with men is not where you want to be. Having a goal creates positive pressure on yourself, which is necessary to move you forward and motivate you to meet men.

Now, I will explain the following steps to goal-setting to meet men.

Step 1- The first step in goal-setting is desire. Desire is the great motivator, the powerful force that drives you toward your goal.

Step 2- The second step is belief - you must believe with all your heart and have no doubts that you have the ability to achieve your goal.

Step 3 - The third and most important step is to write your goal of meeting men in complete detail, exactly as you wish to have it. Until your goal is committed to paper by you, it is not a goal; it is simply a wish backed by perhaps a lot of fantasies.

Step 4 - The fourth step is to determine all the benefits you will receive by achieving your goals of meeting men. Write out on paper all the benefits you will enjoy by accomplishing your goal.

You should really enjoy this step. Just let your imagination run wild and put it on paper.

Step 5 - Step number five is to set a deadline - decide exactly when you are going to accomplish your goal of meeting men and put it on paper.

Step 6 - Step number six is to identify the obstacles you will have to overcome to achieve your goal of meeting men. You will discover that any major obstacles lingering in your mind and preventing you from meeting men will become small when you write them down on paper.

Step 7 – Step number seven is to clearly define the knowledge you need to learn in order to accomplish your goal. All the knowledge you need is right here in this book. Study it and put it into action.

Step 8 - Step number eight is to take all the details that you have identified in step 6 and 7 and make a plan. Be sure and make it complete in every little detail, with all the things you need to do to accomplish your goal.

Step 9 - Step number nine is to get a clear mental picture of your goal as already attained. Picture in your mind over and over, seeing yourself meeting lots of men. Just let your imagination run wild. Become completely obsessed with meeting men in your mind.

Step 10 - Your final step is to back your plan with determination, persistence, and a burning desire to never, never give up until you have achieved your goal.

Here's an example of a written goal:

By _____ (insert date) I will meet and score with a hot & sexy man. I am now going out often and pursuing a relationship with men by every means possible until this goal is accomplished. I'm now taking action when I see an opportunity to meet men. When I go to clubs now, I don't just sit there being passive and just watch other women meet men. I'm aggressive with men now and move into action quickly and easily. It is extremely easy now for me to meet and talk with men, get their phone number, date, and seduce any man I desire.

Signed_____ (your name)   Today's Date _____

This is just an example of what to write for your goal. You can write whatever you want, this is just a guideline. This is very important. Write your goal on an 8 1/2 x 11 piece of paper, preferably blank with no lines. Now, you need to get copies of men's magazines. Cut out pictures of the attractive and sexy men and paste them all around your written goal. When reading your goal, look at these pictures and visualize yourself meeting handsome and sexy men.

Looking at these pictures will work on your subconscious mind and motivate you to reach your goal. Read your goal and look at the photos twice daily. Once when you get up in the morning and once when you go to bed. These are the best times to do this, because your subconscious mind is more receptive to suggestions at this time.

Additional Tips to Help You Achieve Your Goals

1. Focus all of your attention, desire and energy in accomplishing your goal at hand. Forget completely about any consequences of failure with men. Remember that you usually get what you think about most.
2. When you start on your goal, concentrate all of your energy without any distractions on the successful completion of your goal. Make reaching your goal an all-consuming obsession.
3. Develop a self-talk vocabulary to reach your goal of scoring with men. Make it a habit to repeat again and again to yourself, "I want to - I can" in regards to meeting men.
4. Substitute the word "Try" with the word "Will" in your vocabulary associated with meeting men. This is a form of semantics and creates a new attitude of concentrating on things that

you "Will do," instead of things you plan to "Try," with a built-in excuse in advance for possible failure.

5. Substitute the word "Can't" with the word "Can" in your daily vocabulary, too. Always tell yourself you "Can" do things you set your mind to.

In conclusion, set your goals and go for it! Happy Hunting!

Chapter 19 - 100 Ways to Meet Men

1. MOST OF YOU CHIEFLY NEED ENCOURAGEMENT TO TRY. Go out and try to meet men at all of the varied places where men and women come together. Most women who are unsuccessful in love and romance chiefly need ego-bolstering and suggestions of places to look.

2. INDIVIDUAL DIFFERENCES – EVERY WOMAN IS ATTRACTIVE TO SOME MEN. Both men and women who might be considered unattractive to the average person succeed in attracting and winning highly desirable mates every day, every-where. Your own experience will suggest many such cases. Taste and preference in love is infinite. Here is an important fact for you. Believe it and act on it! There is no woman who would not be attractive and desirable to at least some men, including some gorgeous men who would knock your eyes out, and who you ordinarily, though quite foolishly, wouldn't dare to approach.

3. FIND OUT WHAT IMPRESSION YOU MAKE ON MEN. Get an honest and accurate viewpoint from your friends on how you act around men. You just may be coming across as stuck up, sarcastic, domineering, mean, angry, pessimistic, or dull, but once you get a clear picture of how men are seeing you, you can make the appropriate changes.

4. THOUSANDS OF REALLY NICE MEN ARE READY TO GIVE THEMSELVES TO THE FIRST WOMAN WHO IS SENSI-TIVE AND SYMPATHETIC, AND UNDERSTANDING. Loneli-ness, feelings of inner emptiness, a yearning for a sense of personal importance are so universal that millions of nice men, single and married, are psychologically ready to throw themselves, passionately and completely, at the first woman who shows them

tenderness, affection, devotion...at the first woman who makes them feel wanted, loved, important, and lovable!

5. ANY SPECIAL ASSET OR TALENT gives you a higher percentage, but you can succeed in love without any of them, if necessary, provided you have confidence in yourself.

6. MOST WOMEN ARE DEFEATED BY EGO-DEFEATING IMAGINATIONS BEFORE THEY HAVE EVEN BEGUN. The fear that you will not be liked, that you haven't got a chance, that it's no use even trying because "he" could never possibly go for you are your chief, self-imposed obstacles. You use your imagination to erect barriers and obstacles rather than help your cause!

7. A MAGIC FORMULA IF YOU BELIEVE AND PRACTICE IT: A famous, amazingly successful New York psychologist once said during an interview: "I tell all my shy inhibited, introverted patients: Never be afraid to *ask,* you will be surprised and delighted to find out how often you receive a Yes! It is the expectation of receiving a "No" which defeats most women "on the make" before they have half-started."

8. DON'T BE AFRAID TO ASK HIM!

9. A GUARANTEED TECHNIQUE FOR MEETING AT-TRACTIVE MEN EVERY DAY EVERYWHERE. Try this: Make it your business, a self-imposed compulsion and obligation, to talk to at least three attractive, single, men every day wherever you happen to see them, whenever the fancy strikes you. If you want amazing results, don't limit yourself to three. Force yourself to start a conversation, to try and meet a dozen or more men every day, wherever and however you happen to come in contact with them.

10. YOU CAN NOT LEARN MERELY BY READING, YOU MUST GO OUT AND PRACTICE THIS: If you see a man on the street, looking in the window of a store, waiting for a bus, sitting on a train, in the next aisle of a movie, shopping in a department store, and for any reason this man appeals to you, strike up a conversation, start talking to him about anything that comes to mind.

11. HOW DO YOU START A CONVERSATION WITH A STRANGER? If your manner and speech expresses friendliness, openness, lack of ulterior motives, almost any opening or overture on your part will frequently meet with an appreciative response.

By the law of averages, you are certain to come across many men so eager for companionship that they will be happy to respond to you.

12. STARTING WITH WHAT IS "APPROPRIATE" AND "NATURAL": For example, if you are in a movie, what can be more natural than to ask a question about a picture, or make a comment on your reaction to it, or ask the man beside you how he feels about it. If you are on the street, you can always make a comment on something both of you happen to be looking at, or ask for the time, a match, for information on the nearest movie, restaurant, or subway. Then depending upon his reaction, you can always *invite him to join you*!

13. EVEN THE WORLD'S OLDEST PICK-UP LINE OFTEN WORKS. When by chance you approach the right man, almost anything you say will work. Even the oldest, crazy opening line, "Haven't we met some place before?" is used successfully every hour of the day in developing exciting romantic relationships.

14. DO NOT OVERLOOK ANY CHANNEL FOR MEETING MEN. Until you find what you want and are satisfied, you must use every possible and conceivable channel for meeting men. A list of places is suggested in this book.

15. EVERY DATE - EVERY MAN - CAN HELP YOU DE- VELOP MORE SKILL AND POLISH. Every man you meet and go out with can richly add to your experience and self-develop- ment if you look upon it in this way. Don't bury yourself in a movie on the first date. Talk to him about himself; draw out all his interests, desires, crucial life experiences. Share your own experiences with him. From each man you can learn to speak more fluently, with greater ease; you can learn more about the psychology of men; you can develop increasing skill in making him like you and in enjoying your company.

16. MAKE YOURSELF SENSITIVE TO HIS NEEDS. Try to feel and understand just what makes him "tick." Try, occasionally, to put yourself in his shoes mentally and *empathize* with his attitudes and view of life. As you sense unfulfilled needs on his part, really try to satisfy them. Does he want tenderness? Companionship? Boldness? Does he urgently want to get married and will an early subtle indication of serious intentions create the best impression?

17. GIVE FLATTERING ATTENTION PRECISELY WHERE HE MOST CRAVES IT. Does he know he is handsome? Then perhaps he would most appreciate subtle compliments on his intelligence and charm. Is he plain, or suffering from an undeserved sense of inferiority? Then he may most appreciate any compliments which are deft enough to be believable, on the attractiveness of his hair, eyes, physique, or posture.

Explore him and feel him out conversationally, then give flattering attention and appreciation not to his strong points (where he usually does not need it) but on his weak points.

18. LOOK FOR HIS SORE SPOT, HIS UNFULFILLED NEEDS, HIS AREAS OF INFERIORITY OR INADEQUACY, AND STRIVE TO MAKE HIM FEEL GOOD THERE!

19. WHAT IT MEANS TO BE A GOOD LISTENER: A good listener is not really passive. You have to give your fullest, most intense attention to him: physically, mentally, and emotionally; by your facial expressions, posture, your voice and comments. You have to like him and be genuinely interested. Be sensitive enough to discover that every human being has beautiful, lovable inner qualities if you seek for them. Encourage and stimulate the continued flow of his conversation by asking questions, making comments, expressing interest and appreciation for what he is saying. Be ready, too, to contribute your own feelings, experiences, knowledge as it bears upon what he is expressing.

20. IT'S EASY TO BE A GOOD LISTENER IF HE'S VOLUBLE, BUT WHAT IF HE FINDS IT HARD TO CONVERSE EASILY? If he's shy, inhibited, reticent, draw him out. Make him feel important, comfortable, relaxed and appreciated. Your own spontaneity, informality and complete interest in him will bring him out of it.

21. IF YOU NEED TO DEVELOP YOUR OWN SPONTANEITY AND EMOTIONAL FREEDOM, STUDY REFLEX THERAPY BY ANDREW SALTER: Creative Press, NY.

22. THREE BASIC ATTITUDES WHICH FORM A GOLDEN KEY IN ALL HUMAN RELATIONSHIPS IF PRACTICED AND LIVED: Every man wants, unconsciously yearns for, three basic attitudes from the woman he will love. But for that matter, every

human being needs and deserves and will grow in power when he receives these feelings from another person. The formula is: Give a man you desire, *faith, acceptance,* and *respect.* Believe in him, trust him; find the good, beautiful and uniquely admirable within him. Search for it. It is always there! It really makes me sad to think of all the men that are ignored or even dumped prematurely because a woman just did not take the time to get to know him on the inside.

Accept him as he is. This does not mean accepting his pretensions, false fronts or unrealistic goals and dreams. But accept him as he is deep down in his own best and most natural self. Respect him completely in your motives, manners, speech, actions, and plans. If you can truly develop and cultivate these attitudes in yourself, the most desirable men in the world will be eagerly available to you!

23. THE POWER OF "RESPECTFUL AGGRESSIVENESS" IN LOVEMAKING: "He who hesitates is lost!" is often too sadly true of the would-be-lover. Aggressiveness, assertiveness, courage, and persistence are often essential in meeting the man you want and in developing a satisfying love affair. This is not to say that *brutal* aggressiveness or boorish assertiveness is recommended. But you must be aggressive enough to start the action and pursue it, even if given little encouragement initially, unless you are definitely and decisively refused. But that is rare. Don't look for rejection. Don't expect failure! You have to exercise enough assertiveness to keep moving forward, from asking a man for a date, or beginning a conversation with a stranger, through all the successive stages.

24. WHY SOME WOMEN NEVER GET PAST FIRST BASE: Many women with every advantage in looks, personality, and genuine affection of the men they court, never get very far in developing a love affair simply because they do not keep trying, do not keep moving forward. Ignore mild rebuffs, even repeated refusals, unless you are quite certain that the man *really* wants you to stop! Even then, unless he indicates plainly otherwise, you can always try again next time! Remember that most of the time he is only waiting for the opportunity to join you in love and romance, if in the process, you can make him feel secure and appreciated.

25. GOOD ADVICE IS PLENTIFUL - BUT HOW DO YOU TAKE ADVANTAGE OF IT? The advice and ideas contained in this book may be uniquely invaluable to you, but only if you can apply it. There are plenty of other good books and articles which people read, enjoy and ignore! How can you make this advice to change into a more dynamic, effective person with the opposite sex?

26. DON'T JUST READ IT ONCE. No truly worthwhile non-fiction book can be read quickly only once to maximum advantage. You should read, re-read, study, meditate upon, and practice daily, every idea and suggestion in this book which appeals to you.

27. ALL LEARNING IS SELF-DISCOVERY. The human race learned a great deal about the philosophy of effective living thousands of years ago, but each individual must re-discover these truths for herself, make them his own self-discoveries, or they mean nothing to her.

I urge you to re-read and study intensively every word in this book and systematically, persistently, patiently practice it in life, daily, at every possible opportunity. Furthermore, every time you try to meet a man, start a conversation with a stranger, develop a close, affectionate relationship, *and think about* what happened afterwards as this book bears upon what occurred. Analyze for yourself what went wrong, what went right, and try to analyze *why*. Only in this way will you use this book for continuous self-improvement and more effective personal development in finding, attracting, and winning men.

28. OTHER BOOKS CAN HELP IF YOU STUDY AND MASTER THEM. In addition to this book, there are many other books which can be tremendously helpful to you, which can help you more fully understand and appreciate some of the ideas in this book if their fullest significance has escaped you, but you must use them the way we recommend: Study, re-read, master, think seriously about, and practice their advice in life, daily, and persistently.

A Small Sampling of Some of These Helpful Books Follows:

29. HOW TO WIN FRIENDS AND INFLUENCE PEOPLE by Dale Carnegie. This old classic on how to be popular and get along with people is still available in pocket book form in any book store and is a fantastic handbook if you *believe* it and *live* it!

30. FLYING SOLO by Kenneth Wydro. Being single is often a time for self-doubt; but it can and should be a time to grow, to expand, and to soar. Flying Solo proves that the choice is within you to make, and it shows you how it's done: from the bar scene to the job, from your spiritual self to your financial self, from breaking up with style to finding a lifetime mate.

31. CONTACT, THE FIRST FOUR MINUTES by Leonard Zunin, M.D. with Natalie Zunin. This book was written to help you dissolve the distance between yourself and others. One of its main goals is to inspire you to new awareness of who you are and how you present yourself. Through techniques for sensing more about yourself and others you can develop more control over the first four minutes of any contact situation. Your relationships can be warmer, closer, and more significant, if you wish.

32. SHYNESS by Dr. Phillip Zimbardo. Dr. Phillip Zimbardo brings together the results of five years of extensive study, the experiences of more than 5000 people and the startlingly successful techniques of his revolutionary Shyness Clinic to help you face and conquer this life-limiting problem.

33. HOW TO BE SINGLE CREATIVELY by Charles Fracchia. Serves as a guide and a catalyst for the creative experience of living a single life in the fullest possible sense.

34. READ THE BASIC WRITINGS OF SIGMUND FREUD and any other modern psychology books which will help you better understand the dynamics and motivations of human beings, help you understand more sensitively and fully what makes a man tick, and how to sense and gratify his special needs.

35. A PRIMARY PRINCIPLE OF EMOTIONAL HEALTH AND MATURITY. In addition, you should read as many modern books on sex technique as you can get your hands on. You will find at least some helpful things in all of them. But, keep this in mind: if you ever find anything in these books on sex, love, marriage, etc. which makes you feel guilty, ashamed, inadequate or worried about your "normality", either you have grossly misinterpreted the

book or the book contains some real sheer nonsense which you had best disregard!

If you read the enlightened modern books on sex and psychology, you will learn that acceptance of your body and all its functions, and ability to respect, accept and enjoy many avenues of sexual gratification are a primary principle of mental and emotional health and maturity.

36. IF YOU USE THE LAW OF PROBABILITIES, YOU DON'T HAVE TO CHANGE ONE IOTA! If you make it your business to constantly go where and be where many men congregate, and if you put all your efforts into trying to meet and go out with as many men as possible, you will sooner or later meet a man who will fulfill all your dreams and will fall in love with you exactly as you are no matter what handicaps you may think you possess. Individual differences and variations in taste are so great that there are men who are attracted to ugly women, crippled women, fat women, women with eccentricities and peculiarities. If you utilize the law of probabilities of chance and make it your urgent task to meet and go out with one hundred men, for example, long before you have met your one hundredth man, in most cases, you will have found at least one, but more probably, *many* men who will be strongly attracted to you and who will find you irresistible, no matter who you are, no matter what you are like.

37. A FEW TIPS ON SEX APPEAL AND ATTRACTIVENESS FOR WINNING THE CONVENTIONAL MAN. Most ordinary, healthy men are fairly predictable on the constituents of initial sex appeal. These hints are aimed at increasing your percentage with the average man.

Unless you're decidedly beautiful and well-built, you will make a more attractive impression; enhance your sex appeal, if you rely on extreme neatness, cleanliness, and good dress. Even a homely woman with a flabby physique can look proud, popular and attractive if she gives meticulous and expensive attention to being well-clothed. Buy the most up-to-date women's fashionable clothes that you can afford. The cheap ones may fill up your wardrobe but never give you the best break in attractiveness.

You don't have to know anything about clothes really. Go to a clothing store with an excellent reputation and place yourself in the hands of the saleslady. They have enough experience and practice to pick out the kinds of clothes which will make the most flattering combinations for you. Almost every book on salesmanship goes into detail on this facet. You are interested in selling yourself - selling your personality, attractiveness and desirability to men. Take the same advice!

If, however, you are willing to play for the "Law of Probabilities," this advice is less important. If you have outstanding physical and personality assets, it is also far less important.

38. POSTURE AND SEX APPEAL. Posture and manner can contribute greatly to sex appeal, or conversely, diminish it. You may have noticed that some men can appear much more attractive and sexually desirable than their looks alone would warrant because of the sex appeal they convey through posture, voice, smile, vigor of personality. The same is equally true of women.
39. THE WEST POINT MODEL. If you have a sloppy posture, an awkward walk, a slumped, flabby way of carrying yourself, attention to more erect, vigorous, confident, assertive posture can make you many times more attractive and persuasive to the opposite sex. Don't be afraid to practice in front of a mirror. Practice walking with your head up, your chin in, your back erect, your chest as far out as you can push it, and your belly sucked in tight!

Merely standing and walking in this way is terrifically beneficial exercise. But, it is also ever effective in magnifying your sex appeal. Think of the West Point posture as a general pattern model and then develop a posture pattern of your own which is more natural for you, but further in the West Point posture direction than what you possess now.

40. THE POWER OF SETTING GOALS. Every time you give yourself a modest, attainable goal, but one which does require some *effort* and some *courage,* and you accomplish it, you build

another pound of confidence into your bones, flesh and fiber and nervous system - where it must grow and develop if it is to be genuine and durable.

How do you start? Give yourself a small immediate goal and carry it out. Then go on to bigger and better things. If you are afraid of men, go out with any man, and every man, as often as you can. Each time, pat yourself on the back mentally and feel yourself grow more relaxed and secure in the company of men. Set a goal of getting a date with the single man in your place of employment and ask him! Whether he accepts or turns you down, at least be gratified that you were able to carry through, the action of asking him to go out and trying to get a date for yourself on your own.

If you have a phone number in your address book of a single eligible man, call him up and talk to him, ask him for a date. Even if you have never seen him, even if you saw him a long time ago and didn't hit it off, even if he has already refused you, make yourself call him up and try again.

Set yourself a goal of talking to a strange man on the subway, bus, elevator, or street, today! Even if it never gets further than a few casual comments exchanged between you, it will build your confidence and skill and prepare you for more ambitious goals next time. You build confidence by doing things in a small way and forcing yourself forward to gradually bigger and bigger goals.

41. IF EMOTIONAL BLOCKS TO MEETING MEN ARE TOO STRONG FOR SELF-HELP, DON'T BE AFRAID TO TRY PSYCHOTHERAPY OR TRANQUILIZERS. Some of you women who read this may be so shy, inhibited, and psychologically blocked that you will be unable to truly profit from the advice contained in this book. I beseech you not to come to any such conclusion until you have first made a strong, persistent effort to practice these ideas. Remember that the overwhelming majority of people who read this will be able to use this advice effectively without outside professional help.

But if you have powerful blocks, can not bear to start a conversation with a man, or even face the company of a date, no matter how hard you try, then you probably need psycho-therapeutic help.

Get in touch with the nearest mental hygiene clinic, or ask your family physician to recommend a good psychiatrist or psychologist. Your physician may also prescribe one of the many, very effective tranquilizers, not as a cure-all, but to help reduce your anxiety, embarrassment and fear sufficiently for you to begin going out, meeting people, talking to them, and developing promising relationships.

42. YOUR DAILY NEWSPAPER AND BEING AN INTERESTING CONVERSATIONALIST. In addition to being a good listener, a wide-range of interesting topics, comments and humor are helpful in making yourself an attractive, fluent conversationalist with men.

Your daily newspaper can help in this task. Instead of just browsing through it in ten or fifteen minutes each day, read your favorite newspaper from page to page, thoroughly. Read, think about what you are reading, and remember everything of interest and personal importance as you go through each section of the paper. As you read, rehearse in your own mind which items will make an interesting story, an amusing anecdote, a situation which relates to your own and his previous experiences, an item you can modify and include in your repertoire of jokes, witticisms, wisecracks, etc. The human interest stories, even the gossip columns, can often be fruitful sources for vivid, amusing conversation with the appropriate man.

43. LIFE IS FOR NOW! Regardless of the frustrations, failures and grief you may have experienced in the past, there is no reason to permit yourself to be chained to the past, or for that matter, to be so concerned with dreams about the future that the present passes you by.

Life is here, now, this moment...to *live*, to see and feel intensely, to enjoy, to make new starts, new beginnings, build a new life. You can begin actions this very moment which will begin to change you for the better, make you more attractive to, and successful with, the opposite sex. Act, within and without, with friendliness, confidence, and intense interest in others. Like people, even while remaining very open-eyed about their failings and shortcomings. Feel this affection for people inside you and act upon it and you will begin to change internally and externally in a direction which is infinitely more attractive and charming to women.

44. USE IMAGINATION, CREATIVITY AND EMOTIONAL DRIVE IN MEETING AND "MAKING" HANDSOME MEN. Don't rely upon the most convenient, ready at hand methods, sources and techniques. Put some energy, imagination and hard work into the task. Some of the techniques which follow and some of the suggested sources may seem obvious and prosaic when stated in simple, brief form. But it is up to you to go beyond the ordinary, usual approach to these sources for meeting men.

For example, you can go to a dance almost every day and *never dance*, yet still meet dozens of attractive men! Try this: Go up to any man at the dance or nightclub, who is alone and available, as if you were going to ask him for a dance, but instead, in your own words, sincerely, say something like this: "I would love to ask you to dance with me, but I'm not going to because I can't dance! I just had to meet you. Would you mind sitting this one out and just talk and get acquainted?" You will be amazed at how often this works with the most desirable men.

Here are a Few Examples of How Imagination and Courage Can be Applied

45. MEET NEW MEN IN YOUR LOCAL NEWSPAPERS. If you see a picture and a local news item about a man who appeals to you while perusing your newspaper, cut out his picture and the item. In the newspapers of small communities these items can contain the addresses and pictures of attractive, eligible men in connection with every conceivable kind of event. Get the address

right out of the paper and send him a letter introducing yourself and ask if you could get together for lunch or meet for a drink.

If you have some strong obvious ties in common, mention it in your letter, or better yet, just call him up on the phone. For example, if your families know each other, if by chance you went to the same school, if you happen to belong to the same church or organizations, have the same hobbies and interests; use these as stepping stones, as channels to an introduction!

46. GET YOUR CIRCLE OF FRIENDS AND ACQUAINTANCES TO HELP. This, too, often takes some nerve, though less of it than for the above technique but is also very effective. Ask all your friends, acquaintances, associates, relatives, and neighbors, to give you the names, addresses and phone numbers, if not direct introductions, to any and every single man they know. Then call them up or write them, introduce yourself, start a conversation and ask for a date. Be as friendly, warm and informal as you can manage. Try it with persistence. Don't get discouraged five dozen times. By the time you are starting on your sixty-first, you will get marvelous results!

47. GET A PART-TIME JOB WHERE YOU ARE BOUND TO MEET A LOT OF MEN. Even if you now have a very good job, consider trying this: Get yourself a temporary part-time job, evenings, weekends, or whenever you have spare time, regardless of salary or previous background, where you will come into constant contact with men. Department store sales jobs are ideal for this purpose, but almost any selling job, even canvassing can be helpful both in building your confidence in meeting and dealing with people, and in actually giving you more opportunity to meet attractive men from much wider horizons than your own neighborhood or job might provide.

When you get this part-time job, strike up conversations with every single man you meet who interests you. Don't worry about your job or your earnings. You aren't doing the work for a living or a future career anyway. Use the job in a way which will help you develop constant new sources of male contacts.

Here Are 29 Additional Ways of Meeting Men

48. TAKE ADVANTAGE OF DANCES IN YOUR COMMUNITY. Square dances are particularly useful because everyone seems to be a little bit more relaxed, comfortable, and in small country towns everybody knows everyone, and so this is not like the big city nightclubs where people are uptight, so the greater informality makes it easier for you to meet someone. But, don't forget that most men come to dances to meet women and not necessarily to dance. You really do not need to know how to dance to meet many attractive, available men at dances.

49. PARTICIPATE IN COMMUNITY CHEST DRIVES AND COMMUNITY ACTIVITIES OF ALL KINDS. Offer your services. You will meet fellow solicitors; you will meet people on your calls.

50. ATTEND ADULT EDUCATION CLASSES. Some lonely, bored, frustrated men go there to meet women or to escape from their daily routine, than go there to learn.

51. JOIN A POLITICAL CLUB in your community. Have you seen all those available men at campaign rallies and political conventions? Become active politically, on the local level, and you can meet desirable men.

52. MEET NEW FRIENDS THROUGH CORRESPONDENCE. Pen pals and correspondence clubs are pleasant ways to meet men from an almost unlimited source. You can practically have your pick of any part of the country and any "ideal type" you have in mind. You can answer ads or place your own in magazines and tabloids.

53. If you live in a rural area, participate in GRANGE MEETINGS to develop friendships.

54. If you play GOLF or you are willing to learn how, you can go to public links where you can be matched in foursomes of both sexes. Combine health, fun and man-chasing!

55. Most people meet and marry others who have a great deal in common. You can seek out a NATIONALITY ORGANIZATION in your area. Are you of Irish, Greek, or Italian descent? You will be welcomed in a Nationality Club of your choice.

56. BOWLING has become an effective and universal means for men and women to meet. Look into joining a bowling league where the teams are made up of both males and females.

57. GET IN THE SWIM. Be sure, whatever you do, to visit the indoor pools in the winter and even more important, visit the outdoor pools in the summer. If you're good, there's always an attractive man who wants to improve his stroke. In the water, formality is dropped. It's easy to get acquainted. Take my word for it; people tend to be friendlier in the water. So, take advantage of this fact and approach men.

58. BECOME A RED CROSS VOLUNTEER. Help during drives, serve in hospitals, and teach first-aid courses to others. Widen your circle of friends.

59. JOIN A LOCAL AMATEUR BAND OR ORCHESTRA if you play an instrument. People who work together or play together become good friends.

60. Join in good times with your fellow sports enthusiasts by greater participation in ROLLER SKATING and ICE SKATING.

61. There are opportunities for social as well as spiritual betterment at CHURCH-SPONSORED socials, fund drives, the choir, etc.

62. MUSIC LOVER? Attend free municipal concerts. Also get tickets to any private concerts in your area. During intermission you can discuss the program with attractive men who share your interest. You can try to sit beside unescorted men who will happily exchange comments - which may lead to phone numbers and dates.

63. There is something about TRAVEL away from home which makes both sexes friendlier, less inhibited, more aggressive in going after anyone who attracts them. If you can arrange it, take trips by plane, ship, bus...leave your car at home!

64. INTERESTED IN THEATER? Amateur theatrical groups are usually easy to join if you can act, build sets, sell tickets, write scripts, operate lights, etc.

65. In most large cities, your newspapers or yellow pages list MARRIAGE BROKERS who introduce romance-seekers for a fee.

66. JOIN A HOBBY CLUB. If you play cards, chess, checkers, you will find public and private clubs where you can spend enjoyable evenings and meet pleasant partners of both sexes.

67. If this activity appeals to you, join a HIKING, BICYCLING, OR HOSTEL CLUB in your area. Overnight trips, robust fun, informal social fun! You really get to know each other by sharing an activity and romances can be formed.

68. HOW ABOUT A VACATION RESORT? There are combinations to fit any pocketbook. Many single men and women go to resort hotels in their states only for the weekends. You can go to Florida and the Catskills; to Las Vegas or New England, etc. Frequent weekends at the same hotel will make you feel at home with a large crowd of new friends.

69. Make friends on the trail through HORSEBACK RIDING. If you don't know how, consider taking lessons.

70. How long has it been since you had a large FAMILY REUNION? You can meet new distant relatives or induce relatives to introduce you to attractive single eligible men they know.

71. VOLUNTEER your services to CIVIL DEFENSE ORGANIZATIONS which have become increasingly more active and urgently need help.

72. Check your newspapers and phone books for PROFES-SIONAL SOCIAL CLUBS which introduce people and arrange get-acquainted parties as a business.

73. Get yourself a racquet and meet friends on the TENNIS COURTS!

74. If you like to paint, or have always wanted to learn, join a PAINTING GROUP or club...You'll find sexes, all ages, and all types of wielding brushes.

75. LOOK INTO OTHER HOBBIES. Look into your own interests. Read hobby magazines. Find a hobby group in which you can cultivate a new or old interest and meet many men interested in similar pursuits.

76. LOOK INTO OTHER SPORTS. For example, archery, gymnastics, volleyball, competitive diving, ping pong, boating, etc. If you are good at one, you will be attractive to other participants of the opposite sex. You will have a natural common interest on the basis on which friendships, even lifetime matings, may develop.

Here Are Some Suggestions on Technique, Personality, and Miscellaneous Hints:

77. HOW TO CHARM ANY MAN INTO FALLING IN LOVE: There are women who have such winning personalities, such conquering charm, that they can practically seduce a "blind date" over the phone. By analyzing both women who most, and women who least, possess the vital ingredient of "sex appeal" charm, we can present a few of the principles by which it is done. However, this doesn't mean you can equal their charm overnight merely by reading about it. You will have to find your own ways, develop your own brand of charm, and utilizing these principles in a manner which is both polished, and convincing for you.

78. Make the man feel that he's the most important person in the world.

79. Make him feel like he's worth a million dollars.

80. Make him feel attractive, gorgeous, wanted, and sexy.

81. Shower him with attention.

82. Keep talking to him about himself. Forget about yourself.

83. DON'T EVER LEAVE HIM ALONE! Send him cards, flowers, candy, telegrams, gifts, phone him constantly; see him as often as possible until you achieve your objectives.

84. SHOW HIM THAT YOU CARE, DEEPLY, INTENSELY, FOR ALWAYS by the way you look at him, talk to him, pursue him, and listen to him.

85. STRIVE TO MAKE HIM FEEL GOOD whenever he is in your presence, when talking with you, and when out on a date. This means showing him a good time, telling him jokes and interesting anecdotes, expressing appreciation of his sense of humor and behaving as if everything he utters is a bright gem.

86. MAKE HIM DEPENDENT UPON YOU. Make him miss you when you are not around. Teach him to find you more and more essential by being a real friend, an interesting and dependable companion, a reliable antidote to loneliness, a continuous part of his life and thought.

87. MEET HIS FAMILY as soon as possible and treat them as if they were royalty. Get his family on your side in persuading him of your charm and desirability.

88. OCCASIONALLY BE UNPREDICTABLE! Many men, however much they value reliability and security in their woman, also tend to take for granted, and to undervalue a woman who is

too ordinary, too conformist, and too dependably predictable. Don't do it too often, and don't hurt him needlessly, but occasionally demonstrate unpredictable and unexpected qualities.

Leave at least a slight touch of mystery and romantic secrecy about your innermost self. For example, suddenly take a trip without advance warning and write to him from your temporary distant stopping point. Take him on a date to some place he has never been before and which he could not have expected from your previous behavior. Use your imagination to display other romantic touches of mystery and unpredictability. For another example, you may suddenly send him a present which opens up a completely unsuspected but attractive facet of yourself to his admiring contemplation.

89. LOFTY, DRIVING AMBITION IS ATTRACTIVE TO SOME MEN. Spin beautiful dreams of the future for him, and weave him into them! Express your highest, most dramatic ambitions and goals to him. Express them vividly, as concretely and confidently as possible. Give him the feeling that he will go along with you and share the heights, the glory, the success, and your mutual happiness.

90. WHAT TO TELL HIM ONCE YOU HAVE GAINED HIS RESPECT AND HAVE BEGUN TO MEAN SOMETHING TO HIM. Once a man begins to like you, he usually wants to be told certain things over and over about himself. Sad to say, many frustrated husbands, as well as single men, yearn to hear this from their wives but never do. Even where they are *really* loved they are often grossly insulted by being taken for granted.

Tell him over and over again, as sincerely as you can, in as many different ways as you can phrase it: "He's wonderful. He's the most important person in the world to you. You love him. You want him." Once a man *really likes you*, he never, never tires of hearing these things eternally.

91. HOW TO LEARN "SEX CHARM TECHNIQUE" FROM A MOVIE! Most psychologists would agree that it is far better to *be yourself*, to put your effort into self-improvement and self-

development. But if you are too fearful and depressed by a sense of failure and inadequacy to trust in the cultivation of your own most effective self, you may prefer this idea. It's yours to use or omit as you wish. Many single women have found it extremely effective:

Pick out a movie star (or character in literature) whom you admire and with whom you can identify. Go to all of her pictures (or read and re-read every book about her). When you find this movie idol in a love story where she plays the romantic lead and displays her man-swooning charm to greatest advantage, see that picture over and over again until you have learned and mastered every nuance of her voice, speech, manner, humor, posture, all the elements in her screen personality which contribute to her man-conquering style...and pattern yourself accordingly.

92. PICK OUT A SUCCESSFUL MAN-KILLER IN YOUR CROWD AND STUDY HER STYLE. Don't ask her questions. She probably doesn't know herself how she does it. But try to go on "man-hunting expeditions" with her. Go to dances, nightclubs, parties, the beach, with her. Try to arrange some double dates together. Take advantage of every opportunity to watch her in action and study intensively. Remember to rehearse in your own mind, every line and gesture.

93. KEEP A DAILY JOURNAL FOR NEW IDEAS IN IM-PROVING YOUR OWN TECHNIQUE. If you keep your eyes and ears open, you will see women meet men and interest them, you will read items about how romances and love affairs were started and developed in the daily newspapers, movie magazines, novels, and general magazines.

94. WORK OUT A PERSONAL "LINE" AND TRY IT WITH ENDLESS VARIATIONS. Some women need the support, the crutch of a definite "line" in approaching and winning a man. If you do, give a good deal of thought to this while you are working, reading, traveling. Formulate a number of possibly effective lines in your mind and then sit down with a pencil and paper and write them down. Practice them out loud in front of a mirror until you get just the phraseology which sounds most natural, smooth, spontaneous and attractive. Practice delivering it in private aloud until you can use it as if it has just occurred to you in response to

this particular man. Go out and practice it, but with the freedom and confidence to vary it imaginatively to fit every new situation and man.

95. WHY SOME OF THE SUGGESTIONS ARE CONTRADIC-TORY. You can't be spontaneous and natural, cultivate your own deeper self and also imitate the style of sexy movie stars. Some of the advice on these pages is, of necessity, inconsistent and contradictory. The reason is: You are a unique individual. You have been supplied with a tremendous range of suggestions and ideas. Many will not appeal to you or seem appropriate. Some will seem to be the answer to your prayers. You must feel free to choose any and all which you "feel" can be most valuable, and feel equally free to discard and ignore any and all others which do not seem right for you personally.

96. SOME MEN CRAVE A WOMAN WHO IS DOMINATING AND EVEN A LITTLE BIT CRUEL! We mentioned before the importance of sensitively exploring the unfulfilled needs of the man you have met. At times, in the nature of being just a wee bit unpredictable and complex, you may act dominating, bossy, even slightly sadistic. Watch his reactions closely when you do! If you see a glint in his eyes, a pleasurable submissiveness, as suddenly more positive response to you, you may be dealing with a man who has a masochistic need to be dominated and mistreated. If such behavior comes easy and natural for you, it can be exceedingly effective with such men.

97. JUDICIOUSLY MIX TENDERNESS. According to some psychologists, the need for expressing and receiving *tenderness* is even more frustrated and inhibited than the sex drive. Every man needs and appreciates tenderness, and you need to express and receive it. Practice it. You will also find that the man who wants a strong, dominating woman responds best to a judicious counter-point of tenderness and almost brutal domination.

98. YOU DON'T HAVE TO BE A MAN TO PRACTICE GOOD GROOMING, AND YOU SHOULD REGARD ANY SHAME OR EMBARRASSMENT ASSOCIATED WITH IT AS "SHEER IDIOCY!" Don't be afraid of diminishing your femininity by making yourself more physically attractive to men through good grooming. Styled hair, perfume, deodorant, frequent bathing, daily change of underclothing, use of an effective hairspray to keep

your hair the way you want it to look...all these things generally make almost any woman more physically desirable to the opposite sex. Only a rigid and false interpretation of the male and female role make many females guilty about such fastidiousness.

99. STRIVE TO DEVELOP AND LEARN TO PROJECT A QUALITY OF INTENSE FEELING. A passionate interest in life and people, a quality of "excitement: conveyed by one's enthusiasm and intense involvement with life...a rich savoring of the present moment.

100. OPEN YOUR EYES TO THE UNCONVENTIONAL ATTRACTIVENESS AND SEX APPEAL of the "plain" man next door! Taste in attractiveness and sex appeal is often a purely subjective quality. Many men whose faces and bodies attract no public attention or enthusiasm may exert a provocative, tantalizing, even aphrodisiacal effect upon you personally...if you open your eyes and find those subtle elements in him only you can appreciate and cherish.

Chapter 20 - Prayers to Help You Meet, Date, and Find Mr. Right

If you are not a Christian and do not believe in God or Jesus these prayers and Bible verses will not help you. They will fall on deaf ears because you have turned your back on God and Jesus.

To become a new born Christian I encourage you to say this simple prayer to receive salvation through Jesus and become a Christian:

God in heaven, I come to you admitting that I am a sinner. Right now, I choose to turn away from sin, and I ask You to cleanse me of all unrighteousness. I believe that Your only begotten Son, Jesus, who was born of the virgin Mary, died on the cross to take away my sins. I also believe that He rose again from the dead so that I might be forgiven of my sins and made righteous through faith in Him. I call upon the name of Jesus Christ to be Savior and Lord of my life. Jesus, I choose to follow You and ask that You fill me with the power of the Holy Spirit. I declare right now I am a child of God. I am free from sin and full of the righteousness of God. Thank you, Lord. My life is now completely in your hands and I will live for You who gave Yourself for me that I may live forever. I am saved in Jesus' name. Amen.

Welcome to the family of God! If you know other believers, be sure and share this exciting news with them. Also, join a local Bible-based church to connect and worship with other followers of Jesus Christ.

My Prayer: "Dear God, I know that with you all things are possible and I pray that you will help me achieve my goal of having a new boyfriend. In Jesus name I pray, Amen."

My Prayer: "Dear God, help me not make mistakes on my first dates with men. I want my first date to go smoothly and make a good impression on him so I can have a second date. In Jesus name I pray, Amen."

My Prayer: Dear Jesus, make the plans for my love life and let nothing deter me from seeing them fulfilled.

My Prayer: "Dear God, help me overcome my shyness when I go to nightclubs. I get so nervous, fearful, and anxious when I think about approaching men that I am attracted to. Help me overcome these fears and give me the courage to approach men with a calm, cool, and confident attitude. In Jesus name I pray, Amen."

My Prayer: "Dear God, I pray that I don't make any dumb dating mistakes and blunders that turn men off. In Jesus name I pray, Amen"

My Prayer: "Dear God, help me be a good driver when I'm on a date. I want to be a safe driver and not put my life, my date, and other people's lives in jeopardy. If I commit any of these driving sins help me overcome them. In Jesus name I pray, Amen."

Spiritual Comment and Prayer: These are the two most

important prayers to say when you are dating:

1. When something good happens in your dating life say, "Thank you Jesus."
2. When things are going wrong in your dating life say, "Help me Lord."

My Prayer: "Dear Jesus, help me overcome feeling depressed and feeling sorry for myself when I don't have a man to love in my life. Help me avoid having any pity parties. In Jesus name I pray, Amen."

My Prayer: "Dear God, please help me to be myself when dating and not try to pretend to be someone that I am not. In Jesus name I pray, Amen."

My Prayer: "Dear God, help me avoid being possessive, controlling, and smothering men that I date. I don't want to scare men off by being this way. In Jesus name I pray, Amen"

My Prayer: "Dear God, help me to get over and let go of my past relationships that did not work out. In Jesus name I pray, Amen"

My Prayer: Lord please go ahead of me and prepare the way for me to succeed with men. Remove the obstacles to success that would cause me to fail with men.

My Prayer: "Dear God, please help me keep my ego in check and not depend on my looks to meet and attract men. Keep me from walking around with my nose up in the air thinking I'm God's gift to men. In Jesus name I pray, Amen."

My Prayer: "Dear God, I have a bad habit of using profanity around men and people in general. Please help me refrain from cursing when on a date, especially on a first date. Help me be a lade and treat men with respect. In Jesus name I pray, Amen."

My Prayer: Jesus, fill me with your Holy Spirit and ease my restless mind in anticipation of going on my first date with the man

I'm so crazy about.

My Prayer: Dear God, if I learn that a man I am dating is unfaithful, make sure that I stop dating him and not give him a second chance. As the old saying goes "Once a cheater always a cheater." In Jesus name I pray, Amen."

My Prayer: Dear God, please help me to stop smoking. Help me realize that this habit turns off a lot of men and can interfere with my dating men. More importantly, it can cause me some serious health problems. I want to live a long healthy life. In Jesus name I pray, Amen."

My Prayer: "Dear God, I have a bad habit of thinking all men and people in general should think like I do. Help me realize that we are all unique individuals and all of us don't think alike. In Jesus name I pray, Amen."

My Prayer: Jesus please help me to find good and kind words that will bring cheer to my date.

My Prayer: Jesus, help me to remember that your power can lift me above any setback in my relationships with men.

My Prayer: "Dear God, I want to be a winner in the game of dating, love, and romance. Please help me follow these guidelines to help me win with men. In Jesus name I pray, Amen."

My Prayer: "Dear God, don't let any of my fears of failure with men rear its ugly head in my mind. Keep my thoughts positive and focused on succeeding with men. In Jesus name I pray, Amen."

My Prayer: "Dear God, help me be sympathetic when I'm on a date. Help me refrain from offering solutions instead of being sympathetic and understanding with any problems he may discuss. In Jesus name I pray, Amen."

My Prayer: When success comes my way with men I turn to you Jesus with a heart of thanksgiving.

My Prayer: "Dear God, help me realize that I am responsible for my happiness. Don't let me fall into the mental trap that I must be in a relationship to be happy. In Jesus name I pray, Amen

My Prayer: Dear God, help me develop a game plan for finding the right man for me. Make sure I don't just settle for anyone just to be in a relationship. In Jesus name I pray, Amen."

My Prayer: "Dear God, help me have a positive and upbeat outlook when out on a date with men. Make sure I don't bitch, whine, and complain when I'm on a date because this will turn him off and make him not want to date me again. In Jesus name I pray, Amen."

My Prayer: "Dear God, I have a bad habit of putting things off when it comes to making an effort to meet, date, and attract men. Please help me get off of my dead ass and take action to meet, date, and attract men. Give me the attitude of, "Do it now" instead of procrastination. In Jesus name I pray, Amen."

My Prayer: "Dear God, I have a bad habit of taking control of all of the conversations on my dates. Help me give him equal time in talking and listen intently to what he has to say. In Jesus name I pray, Amen."

My Prayer: "Dear God, help me to not talk about anything sexual when on a first date. He most likely will be offended and may not want to see me again. In Jesus name I pray, Amen."

My Prayer: "Dear God, help me take the time to get to know a man before I fall in love with him. In Jesus name I pray, Amen."

My Prayer: Dear Jesus, please help me improve my posture so I can make a better impression on men. Make sure that I stand straight with my shoulders back. I want to look like a West Point cadet...in Jesus name I pray...amen

My Prayer: "Dear God, help me overcome feeling depressed and feeling sorry for myself when I don't have a man to love in my life. Help me avoid having any pity parties. In Jesus name I pray, Amen."

My Prayer: Dear Jesus, I ask you for a clear direction in my dating life. Guide my steps and show me the way. In Jesus name I pray, Amen.

My Prayer: I have never known a despondent day...It's because the joy of the Lord is the strength of my life.

My Prayer: Dear God, help me overcome my fears in approaching men that are holding me back from meeting men. In Jesus name I pray, Amen.

My Prayer: "Dear God, please help me from getting involved with men who would not be good for me. In Jesus name I pray, Amen"

My Prayer: There is nothing in my life that does not come from you, Jesus. This includes that special man you will send me that seems heaven sent.

My Prayer: "Dear God, help me get over and bury all my negative experiences in dating. I want to forget them and focus on having positive experiences in dating for my future. In Jesus name I pray, Amen."

My Prayer: Thank you Jesus for the unbreakable promise that you hear and answer my prayers for somebody to love.

Bonus Section "How to Talk to Men"

I have included in this book a special free report called, "How to Talk to Men." This in depth report will teach you the art of conversation after you have made contact with a man. Follow this advice and you will become an expert at meeting men and you will never be at a loss for words again when you're around men.

You will learn the secrets to keep exciting, interesting conversation going for hours with men. They will admire you for your conversational skills and this crash course in how to talk to men will make you so popular with men that they will crave to be with you because you know how to talk to them.

The Six Deadly Sins of Conversation with Men

SIN #1 - Bragging about yourself and your accomplishments. There's no faster way of driving men away from you than by constantly talking about yourself and your own great accomplishments.

Forget about yourself. The whole art of conversation with a man is to become interested in him rather than trying to get him interested in you.

Remember that most people are interested in themselves morning, noon, and night. Never forget this fact. After all, why should a man be interested in you unless you are interested in him first? Just put your ego aside and concentrate solely on him and his interests.

SIN #2 - Criticizing him in public. This is a big no, no. Nobody likes to be criticized in front of others. So, if there are others around, refrain from telling him he's dead wrong about things or pointing out a terrible mistake that he has made.

This will make a bad impression on him, especially if you don't even hardly know him. Nobody likes to be embarrassed in front of his or her friends, relatives, co-workers, etc.

SIN # 3 - Making sarcastic remarks and making fun of him. Don't make the mistake of making any sarcastic remarks toward him. Most people don't appreciate sarcasm. Just be optimistic and upbeat towards him no matter what's going on. You'll be a lot better off. And whatever you do, don't make fun of him. If you make fun of him, if you belittle and ridicule him, or if you make a fool out of him, especially in front of others, you'll have him as an enemy for the rest of your life. He will never forget this incident or forgive you. People don't like their ego deflated and their pride hurt. Do the opposite and give him lots of praise.

SIN #4 - Trying to prove to him that you're more intelligent than he is. If you really are a highly intelligent person, just keep it to yourself. Don't try to show how much smarter you are than he is.

Now, I realize that some men may lack formal education, their mentality may have been altered by drugs, a dysfunctional family, or they are somewhat naturally stupid. Forget all this and relate to him on his level.

You will be able to communicate with him much better and if you can't carry on an intelligent conversation with him you are off to a bad start. Also, you may intimidate him by putting his intelligence down. He may not care to be around you and just get up and leave.

SIN #5 - Interrupting him during conversation. This is a quick way of becoming unpopular with him and even being disliked. Interrupting him when he's trying to say something is an insult and can hurt his feelings. If you are doing this it stems from your ego problem of wanting to feel important, to be heard, and to be recognized.

Don't commit this deadly sin and just put your ego aside and concentrate completely on what he is saying. Focus all of your undivided attention on him and don't butt in. Hear him out. If you listen closely enough, you might even learn something of value.

SIN #6 - Not listening to him. Nobody likes to be ignored. Failure to pay attention to him while he is talking is an insult. It is a form of rejection and nobody likes to feel rejected. Don't be preoccupied with what's going on around you and tune him out. Don't focus on other men around you either.

If he's talking about a subject you have no interest in, don't spend your time trying to come up with ways to change the topic of conversation to something that you enjoy talking about. Hear him out!

Don't make this mistake either. Let's say he's talking about a subject you're really interested in and you get so anxious to put your two cents worth in and comments, you spend your time going over in your mind what you are going to say rather than listening attentively to him.

5 Steps to an Introduction to Men

Here's the basic way of introducing yourself to a man that you are attracted to. Let's say that your name is Susan Evans.

1. Move to within two to three feet of him, the most comfortable conversational distance.
2. Smile.
3. Focus your eyes on the bridge of his nose. This is tantamount to eye contact, but is easier to maintain.
4. Hold out your hand.
5. "Hi, you look nice. My name is ...." Almost always, he will shake your hand and introduce himself. They'll be favorably impressed with your approach, indeed pleased that you came up to them. Your response then should be, "Nice to meet you...," using the person's name.

What to Say to Him Next

After you've introduced yourself to him and exchanged names, in most social situations you can make a remark in which you do two things:

1. Pay him a compliment. Express something you like about what he is doing, wearing or saying. The feeling you seek to convey is, "I'm positive. I support you. You can relax with me."
2. Ask a question. It should be related to the compliment you just gave. Your underlying message: "I'm interested in getting to know you better." For example, you might say: " You sure look nice today."

Ask Him for Advice

Another good ice-breaker: Ask for advice. Most people are flattered when they're asked for recommendations. Almost as good as asking for information. People usually like to be consulted. You could ask him "Where's a good romantic restaurant to eat at?" or "I need to buy my father some nice cologne, can you recommend a good brand?"

Ask Him Open-Ended Questions

Some questions require only a yes/no or other short answer. Those are called "closed-ended" questions. The man answers. Then, unless more information is volunteered, the conversation goes nowhere. Generally, you elicit more interesting responses with "open-ended" questions. These essay-type questions encourage him to reveal facts, opinions, and feelings. Focus on open-ended questions, which often start with "How....?" "Why....?" and "What?" If you ask closed-ended questions, you can invite the person to elaborate by following with questions like: "In what way?" "For example?" "How do you mean?"

Share with Him What's on Your Mind

When you know some of his "hot buttons" - the things that are important to him can be a source of extended conversation. Also reveal your own enthusiasms to him. By letting him know what's important to you, you are giving him an opportunity to get to know you in a way that you want to be known. When you talk about events that are important to you, he will get an idea of your personality, and it also provides an enormous source of conversational material.

Take an Inventory of Yourself

Before you'll be meeting new men, take an inventory of the things that are important to you, and that you'd like to talk about. What are you excited about now? What changes are taking place in your life? What have been the most important events or people in your life? What future plans are you most enthusiastic about? Why do you feel the way you do about things? What are your concerns? What is your vision for the future? What are your likes and preferences? The answers to these questions tell him how you relate to the world around you. Be specific, so that your conversational partner gets a lot of free information to pick up on. Communicate your enthusiasm. Disclose some of your feelings and values.

Some Fall-Backs for Shy Women

If you're shy and have trouble talking to men, it helps to be prepared with things to talk about. Besides the things that are most important to you, here are sources for conversational fuel:

1. Come up with 3 or 4 interesting or exciting things that have happened to you recently. Practice telling these stories on family or friends, or practice in front of a mirror or with a tape recorder.
2. Read current newspapers and magazines, and be prepared to talk about events that interest you.
3. Collect a couple of sure-fire, inoffensive jokes.
4. Become knowledgeable about what's going on in your city. People always want to know more about what's happening locally.
5. See current movies and read current books. You're bound to find men who have seen the same movies or read the same books.

Give Him Good Feedback

Occasionally nod and make remarks to show him you are paying attention and understand what is being said. "Mm hm....Oh yeah....right....go on...."

To encourage him you can also say, "Why do you say that?" "In what ways?" "How so?" Echoing is another technique of active listening: He says, "I just bought me a new mustang convertible." You say, "A new mustang convertible, that's great!"

Don't Worry - Listen to Him!

Don't worry about what you should say to him next. While you're thinking about this, you aren't listening! You'll know what to say by listening carefully for keywords, main ideas, facts, opinions, and feelings. Listen most of all for free information on which to base questions. If you are told, "I was in Las Vegas just last week to party and do some gambling, you can offer information about yourself: "Oh, I was brought up in Las Vegas!" or "I enjoy gambling too." You can also ask:

"Do you enjoy going to Las Vegas?"
"Were you brought up in the Las Vegas area?"
"Where do you like to go in Vegas?"
"What kind of gambling do you enjoy in Vegas?"

Restate In Your Own Words

Listen to what he is saying, decide why it is being said, and then restate it in your own words. For example, if he tells you, "women are always hitting up on me, propositioning me, or asking me to go home with them, you might say, "it sounds like you're getting tired of being treated like a sex object."

It's best to restate occasionally, after he has expressed a particular point. You can restate by saying, "So what you mean is...." or "Now if I understand you correctly...." Summarizing in this way makes you listen carefully and lets him know if the message was communicated correctly, and eliminates any misunderstandings.

People often stray from the main topic. As a listener, it is helpful for you to keep this central idea in mind, and from time to time put the conversation back on track. Summarizing will allow you to do this. You can say, "It sounds to me like you are saying....Am I right?"

Use and Ask For Examples

Examples are important for clarifying what is being said and for making conversation more vivid and memorable. Use examples to support what you are saying, or to question what you are hearing, and ask for examples whenever you are unsure of his point.

Conversation Pitfalls

When talking about things that excite and interest you, here are some pitfalls you'll want to avoid:

1. Don't dominate the conversation with your own enthusiasm. Be sensitive to how much time you devote to your own subject without hearing again from the other person. It's alright to let him know what turns you on, but be aware that he may not necessarily want to hear everything you have to say about that topic.
2. Avoid Jargon or technical terms when discussing topics with him and he isn't familiar with the subject. You can give him an inside look at what excites you about the topic, rather than overly specific details.
3. Be careful not to lecture or try to "sell" him on what you believe in; regardless of how strongly you believe in it or how important you feel it is. He may want to learn more about a subject that interests you, but they don't necessarily wish to be converted to your point of view.
4. Don't tell personal secrets in the early stages of a friendship with a man. Of course, it's flattering to him to be told something confidential, but if this is early on in a friendship, the person is likely to think, "If she tells me such personal things right off, she probably tells everyone." Wait until the time is right, and you've established trust.
5. Don't try to override his point of view with your superior knowledge of a subject. Be receptive to his point of view and listen to what he has to say. Then, when it's your turn to give your opinion, he will be more receptive and open to your ideas.

Be Sensitive to His Responses

If he gives you a brief response, he may not wish to discuss the topic for a particular reason. Be sensitive to unenthusiastic responses, and be ready to change to a new topic quickly when you feel you have touched on a high-sensitivity or low-interest area for him.

Avoiding Sensitive Topics

What do you do if he brings up a subject that you feel is inappropriate? These are subjects that are in poor taste or which may make you feel uncomfortable - a racial slur, for example.

You can show that you don't share this opinion, but without making a fuss about it. You might simply say, "I don't really agree with that," or "I'm sure we can find more pleasant things to talk about." Now, since you made the suggestion to change the subject, it's up to you to do just that. Pick up the conversational ball quickly and open a new topic of discussion by making a comment or asking an open-ended question based on free information that you heard earlier.

Keep Your Ears Open

An iceberg statement is a piece of free information in which 90 percent is under the surface, waiting to be asked about. These statements are hints of what he would really like to talk about.

An example is "Oh, thank you. I got that shirt when I was on vacation in Mexico." The speaker wants you to ask a follow-up question: "When were you in Mexico?"

People are usually hesitant to compliment themselves. He may complain to you that none of his clothes fit anymore because they're too big. If you are a sensitive listener, you may realize he is really telling you he has lost weight and would like to be congratulated. Be alert for such clues.

Watch Your Timing

Be sure your timing is good. Imagine you are being given an explanation of how to slow cook a roast. "Then you slow-cook the roast in a crock pot." If you don't know what a crock pot is, now is the time to ask. If you wait until the recipe is completed before asking, "What is a crock pot?" you come across as an uncaring listener.

Asking a question at the appropriate time shows you are listening to him and understand what is being said. In contrast, if you are told all about his trip to Hawaii and at the end of the story ask, "So where did you stay when you first got there?" You will come across as an insincere listener, someone who is asking out of politeness and not paying attention. Remember, if you listen carefully and concentrate on what he is saying, you will be able to ask the right questions at the right time.

Give Him Your Own Information

It isn't enough to give him plenty of opportunities to talk by constantly asking questions. It can become draining to be asked question after question without learning anything about him and it can begin to feel like an interview. When you ask questions, include some information about yourself. Rather than asking, "Where were you brought up?" You might say, "I was born in Nevada but I lived in California from the time I was a year old until I went to college. Did you grow up on the West Coast?"

This ensures that you will both get something out of the conversation, while you show your interest and make the person who is being asked questions more comfortable.

Animate Your Listening

He can't read your mind, but he can read your face to get a clue of your reactions. Look at yourself in a mirror and imagine things that make you sad, happy, astonished, and shocked.

Exaggerate your expressions - try so hard that every facial muscle feels strained!

Experiment with every feeling you think may come up in a conversation - respect, admiration, and sympathy. As you become more used to expressing your emotions this way, you will feel less as though you are overdoing it, and you will better convey your feelings.

Learn To Change the Topic

Learning how to gracefully change the topic is one of the best ways of keeping a conversation going. It also provides an opportunity for you and him to find areas of mutual interest.

A Flowing Conversation

A good conversation flows in and out of several topics. People jump from point to point. A remark may spur a recollection about a completely different matter. Then the talk may naturally flow back to the original topic. You shouldn't feel that you have to completely exhaust all the possibilities of one topic before proceeding to the next.

Picking Up On Free Information

In looking for ways to change the topic, be attentive for free information - remarks that are made in passing, and that you can later pick up on.

If the person has mentioned just returning from a trip, for example, you have many opportunities to bring the conversation back to various aspects of travel. "What sort of accommodations did you have in Hawaii? Do you prefer big hotels, or condos?" "Have you done much traveling in the Caribbean?"

This topic also allows you to contribute your own information on the topic. "I was in Hawaii last year." Be sure to reveal plenty of free information about yourself throughout the conversation. This helps him pick up on subjects for later in the conversation.

When it seems to you that a subject is getting sluggish, change it by referring to some free information revealed earlier. Or else offer some new information of your own.

You might say, "It's interesting to hear you talk about Lake Mead because my favorite thing to do is to rent jet skis on Lake Mead." You might also refer back to a previous topic by saying, "I heard you mention earlier...."

Ask Him a Ritual Question

If the topic you've been discussing seems to be on the verge of dying, one way of changing topics is to ask a ritual question. You might say, "You said you've been in Florida for three years. Where were you before then?" Sometimes you might want to change to another topic for only a brief moment. All you have to do is say: "Excuse me, but I'd like to change the subject for a moment," and then make your comment or ask your question.

Try to complete your ideas quickly and then return to your original topic of discussion. Don't do this too often. You may give the impression that your mind is scattered, or that you cannot (or don't care to) discuss a particular topic on a meaningful level, and therefore are avoiding the topic. It may also suggest that you are not listening or that you are bored with the subject matter.

Make Use of Names

Repeat his name several times as you speak. That will help you remember it. Moreover, using his name is one of the easiest and most meaningful compliments you can give. You might find it easier to remember names if you visualize them written out. Ask how to spell a difficult name. If you happen to forget his name, it's perfectly OK to say, "Forgive me, but tell me your name again." Don't be embarrassed.

Focus On Him

Give him your undivided attention. Focus your ears as well as your eyes on him as he speaks. If you practice techniques such as restating and echoing, it is less likely your mind will wander. If your mind does wander, don't try to guess what you missed.

Admit that you must have missed something, and ask him to repeat it.

As you become a more experienced conversationalist, it will be easier for your mind, senses and emotions to clear themselves of distractions. You'll do a better job of hearing what he has to say when you can concentrate more freely.

Listen To Him without Judgment

While you're listening to him, focus on his point of view. Try to suspend emotions and judgment temporarily and soak up information without bias. Try to listen objectively. How can you respond intelligently unless you know exactly what the other person is saying?

Use Body Language

Maintaining eye contact, keeping your arms unfolded, and leaning slightly forward indicates your interest. Imagine you are telling a man about your exciting new job. He has his arms crossed in front of him, and he is staring beyond you at women across the way.

Does he seem interested in what you have to say? Is he blocking distractions and concentrating on what you're saying and how you feel? He probably won't have very many successful conversations because his body language tells people he is closing himself to them. Good body language gives the speaker the message you're curious and attentive.

Nod in Your Conversations

In conversations, nod while he is speaking. Slow, repeated nodding indicates general affirmation. Your nodding shows that you understand what's being said. It says, "Yes. Go on." - and invites him to continue speaking. Add to your physical vocabulary quick nodding, to show, "Ah yes, I understand!"

Avoid a Rigid Head Around Men

Avoid having a rigidly held head and stiff neck. In body language such a stance is a conversation killer, especially if combined with a blank facial expression. By contrast, if you get into the habit of nodding, you'll encourage continued contact.

Lean Forward While Listening To Him

Lean forward slightly while he is talking to you. You'll show that you're listening and interested. He will feel complimented, and will feel encouraged to continue talking. Refrain from leaning back with your hands behind your head. That posture gives off messages of judgment, skepticism, and boredom - and will inhibit him from speaking.

Keep the Right Distance When Approaching Men

Place yourself within about 5 feet of the man you want to attract. That's a comfortable distance to start a conversation. As you speak, move closer. The preferred conversational distance for most Americans is about 2-1/2 feet. For an intimate conversation, you might move to 2 feet. Closer than that, and you'd best be on intimate terms with him. Beware moving too close too soon. If you violate people's "personal space," they're likely to consider you pushy and back away from you.

The Eyes Have It with Men

Use your eyes as well as your mouth. Gaze into his eyes as you smile at him. It will make your message much more personal. When you see men who look interesting, turn toward them and let your gaze linger a little longer. A suggestion of a wink while you're smiling gives an unmistakable come-hither look.

Rules of Conversation

In conversation, look into the eyes of the man you're talking with. Direct eye contact says, "I'm listening. I want to hear more." To show agreement and interest, occasionally raise and lower your eyebrows. When he's talking, listen with your eyes as well as your ears. If you look away, you may signify, "I'm bored" or "I don't agree." The result will usually be a short and unfulfilling conversation. However, to look away while speaking is natural. It's a sign that the topic is being shifted or that thoughts are being collected. A pause while glancing away usually means an incomplete thought, signaling, "I haven't finished. Don't interrupt."

Are Your Eyes Right With Men?

Be cautious lest your eye gestures be misunderstood. Avoiding eye contact can make both parties feel uncomfortable. If you avert your eyes out of shyness, you may be interpreted as saying, "I'm dishonest" or "I'm ashamed" or "I'm not interested in you." Too much eye contact is as bad as too little. It's impolite to stare. As a cultural rule, a woman should not look steadily at a man for longer than a few seconds - unless he gives her license with a smile, a backward glance, or a direct meeting of eyes. When a woman gazes without smiling, men may think, "She's undressing me with her eyes" or "She's looking right through me." If you narrow your eyes in a frown, you may inadvertently be saying, "I'm suspicious." If you roll your eyes upward, he could think you're yawning, "Ho hum!" If you glare at a man under arched eyebrows, most men will hear you growl: "I'm angry."

Work Up To It

It can be difficult to gaze into a man's eyes. To get used to making eye contact, focus your gaze a little below or between his eyes. For a few seconds look into the pupils, and smile. To ease the tension, look into one eye at a time. To relax, let your gaze travel over the features of the face: the lips, cheeks, nose, ears and hair. After a few moments, go back to looking at him right in the eyes.

From time to time, ask yourself, "Where are my eyes?" Out of habit, you may find your gaze has drifted onto the floor or out in the audience. Increase the amount of time that you experience direct eye contact. As you become more practiced, you'll be able to look directly into his eyes without even being conscious that you're doing it.

Explore Common Interests with Him

Let's say you met a man, you talked a little, and it seems to you that you could get to be friends. You're attracted to each other, the atmosphere is positive, and you've found some areas of common interest. Now's the time to explore other areas of common interest, and to build on the ones you've already discovered.

Make Quick Connections

It's not rude to make small interjections into a conversation to let him know when another area of common interest has been hit upon. For example, if he tells you he's exploring taking skiing lessons, you might interject a quick comment: "Oh, good. I did that last year." A quick question is another possibility. It serves the purpose of keeping the conversation going, while also reinforcing common interests. "Oh, I've thought about taking skiing lessons myself," you might say. "Can you tell me more about it?"

Quick inserts provide him with immediate feedback and let him know that you can relate to the subject. You might also signal when you agree with a judgment - about a movie or concert. You might quickly put in, "It's nice to know I'm not the only one in the world who hated the movie, Four Weddings and a Funeral. The critics must have seen a different version." If you don't let him know that you relate to several details of his conversation, then you may lose many areas of fruitful conversation. These identified areas of common interest also come to your aid if the conversation dies. You can go back to areas of mutual interest and pick up on a point you'd like to know more about. "About the time you lived in New York City, was it really a terrible place to live?"

Picking Up On Information

When you make connections with his experience, you also give him free information to pick up on. He might, for example, go back to the conversation about skiing and ask about what you learned about skiing. Remember that most people have many interests, and they want to find which interests you have in common. Each bridge that you build gives you the opportunity to return for more conversation. The more bridges you build, the more you will be able to share with one another. When you meet a man and discover areas of common interest and experience, you gain building blocks to develop a deeper relationship.

The Next Step

Once you've discovered an area of mutual interest and have begun to explore it, you have a natural reason to see each other again. If you discover a shared interest in camping, it's natural for one of you to suggest going camping together. If you're both interested in taking the same cooking course for example, it might be reasonable for you to share transportation and go out for coffee afterwards. The more interests, experiences and outlooks you share, the more likely it is that you'll be able to develop a solid and rewarding friendship that can lead to an intimate affair.

Ask Him Follow-up Questions

Ask follow-up questions based on details he mentions. Direct your conversation into areas of mutual interest. If you comment on his ring and he says in passing that he bought it in Mexico, you know you can ask about his trip to Mexico: Where he stayed, what he did, what you might find interesting.

Are You Prying Too Much?

Most men expect to answer easy, straightforward questions when they first meet women. Such questions are part of the ritual of becoming acquainted. What's more, he's likely to be complimented by your show of genuine interest. From initial, impersonal topics, you can then go on to discuss personal backgrounds and interests. By exchanging details about yourselves, you can get to know each other quickly - and determine if you'd like to pursue the contact, perhaps.

When might a question be too personal? Practice will help you develop sensitivity to what sort of questions men are glad to answer in various stages of a relationship. If you have any doubts about whether a question is appropriate, preface it with a statement like: "May I ask if....?" or "If you don't mind telling me...." or "I hope I'm not being too personal...." If he doesn't feel pressured to reply, they'll usually respond cordially to the extent they're comfortable.

How to Respond To Questions

If you're on the receiving end of questions, volunteer plenty of information about yourself for him to pick up on. Talk about your work, interests, plans, feelings, and hopes. Your full answers will show you're an open person who's easy to talk to. Such details of your everyday life are fascinating to other people. If you withhold basic facts about yourself, he may become bored or suspicious, and lose interest in trying to know you.

Handling Personal Questions

On the other hand, you may be asked questions that are too personal for this stage of your relationship. The simplest way of responding is to not answer. Generally, your silence will quickly be filled in by his comment. If pressed for an answer, you can change the subject. Or reply, "I'd rather not say" or "I've been asked not to talk about that." If he persists in invading your privacy, you're better off not knowing him.

Avoid Second-Guessing Him

You can think faster than you can speak. Therefore, it is tempting to listen for a few moments and then attempt to guess what point is being led up to. "You'll never believe what happened this morning," someone tells you excitedly. "I was driving to work. I looked in my rear view mirror " - "And there was a cop pulling you over," you interrupt. The speaker's face falls. "Well, no. I was just going to say that there was a guy riding in the car behind me mooning me."

It's Insulting

It is an acceptable mental exercise to try to anticipate what will be said, but to verbalize it (second-guessing) is insulting. Even worse, you may be wrong. It is also best to refrain from completing sentences when he pauses to construct his words. You don't have to agree with everything he says in order to be a good listener. Just give him time to express himself before you add your opinion.

Listen and Reflect

Whenever you have the urge to disagree, judge or interrupt him, listen instead and reflect on what you hear. Remember the importance of asking a question when it is relevant, and avoid interrupting and completing sentences. A good conversation includes ample give-and-take, but skills are necessary and invaluable.

Keeping Conversations Going With Him

After you've been approached by him or approached him and chatted for a few minutes, what next? You've asked a few ritual questions, found out a little about him and shared a little about yourself, but how do you sustain a conversation?

Many women clam up at this juncture. To help you keep a conversation going, here are some tips:

Focus On the Situation at Hand

Your most obvious subject for a sustained conversation is the situation you both find yourselves in. You hardly need to think of what to say next. Simply tune into your immediate surroundings. Observe your situation and find something to ask or comment about. Share your reactions to what is taking place at the moment.

Relate your thoughts and feelings about the situation you find yourselves in, and about his reaction to it.

Direct Your Thoughts Outward

Try to direct your thoughts outward instead of inward. If you're concentrating too much on your own reactions, you may tune in to your own uneasiness or panic - instead of what he is saying.

Show a real interest in what he is saying. To be interested is to be interesting.

By directing your thoughts outward to him and your surroundings, this will keep you from worrying how you look, what he thinks about you, whether he likes you and thinks you're attractive and intelligent, etc. Such self-conscious preoccupations can get in the way of keeping the conversation going.

Discover the Big Events in His Life

One sure-fire way to keep a conversation rolling is to discover the big events in his life - the things that are meaningful to him, and which he is anxious to talk about. I call such areas of interest "hot buttons."

A hot button is a subject that really interests you and him and that you can talk about for an extended period of time. A hot button can be a lifelong interest, a passing fancy, or a current fascination - whatever turns you on!" Hot buttons can be work, a new job, a hobby, a career goal, an upcoming trip, a sporting activity, whatever.

Finding His Hot Buttons

In conversations with new men you meet, try to find their hot buttons as soon as you can.

These strong interests are extremely fertile areas for sustained conversations, particularly if you discover that you share some strong interests.

To find his hot buttons, fish around subject areas with ritual questions. When you receive an unusually enthusiastic response, chances are you've hit on a particular interest. Pursue the subject by indicating some interest in it.

Balance Talking and Listening to Him

Be aware, as you engage in conversation, of balancing the exchange. In a good conversation, partners take turns talking. When a conversation is over, you should feel that neither of you dominated the conversation, that you had roughly equal time. That way, you get to know each other at about the same rate.

Good conversation is a balance of talking and listening. If the conversational ball has been in your court for some time, make a point of tossing it back to him.

If you're presenting a complicated idea, give the broad outlines first, and then wait for feedback before you go into the details. Otherwise, you may inadvertently hog the conversation for longer than you realize.

The more balanced your exchanges are, the more quickly you'll really get to know him and the more likely the relationship can progress.

Buy Our Books on Amazon

How to Improve Your Golf with S/A Hypnotism - Golf buddies will stare in amazement at great shots you make. Go to: www.amazon.com and type don diebel in the search box.

How to Use the Power of Jesus to Help you Meet, Date, and Attract Men - Featuring 179 spiritual inspirations and advice for dating men, 145 must-read Bible verses to help you succeed with men, and 50 powerful prayers to help you overcome any problem you will ever have in dating men. To buy go to: www.amazon.com and type don diebel in the search box.

About the Author Don Diebel

I'd like to introduce myself: I'm Don Diebel (America's #1 Single's Expert) and one of the nation's leading experts on dating and relationships, guest speaker on several TV and radio shows, featured in print interviews, dating consultant, and I have helped thousands of both men and women win at the game of love with my phenomenal best-selling books, dating articles, and dating advice at: www.getgirls.com

First of all, I'd like to say that we were all put on this earth for a reason and purpose. I feel that I was put on this earth to help men and women succeed with the opposite sex. Let's face...It's a jungle out there in the dating world for many, the search for love and romance continues to be frustrating, unfulfilling, lonely, and heart breaking.

Also, their fear of rejection, lack of confidence, shyness, and fear of catching AIDS, herpes, and venereal diseases creates what seems like insurmountable obstacles to meeting men. And for those women who actually do go on dates, many of them never even get a second date with the men they desire.

Affiliation: Doctorate of Publishing - Presented by Para Publishing - November 6, 1988.

Graduate of the Key West College of Millionaires - October 11, 1990.

I am the author of the following best-selling books:

The Complete Guide to Meeting Women...Featured in the Playboy Catalog and on the Jimmy Fallon Tonight Show

How to Pick Up Women in Nightclubs

1001 Best Pick Up Lines...Sure-Fire Opening Lines for Meeting, Dating, Attracting, and Seducing Women

200 Guaranteed Ways to Succeed with Women...Everything You Need to Know on How to Meet, Date, and Attract Women

The Houston Entertainment and Dating Guide

How to Pick Up Women in Discos

How to Improve Your Golf with S/A Hypnotism

Finding Mr. Right

100 Places to Take a Date

Dating with Jesus...A Daily Spiritual Guide for Men On How to Meet, Date, and Attract Women

How to Use the Power of Jesus to Help You Meet, Date, and Attract Men

How to Use the Power of Jesus to Help You Meet, Date, and Attract Women

Help Me Jesus: 365 Daily Spiritual Devotions to Help Men Meet, Date, and Attract Women

www.ingramcontent.com/pod-product-compliance
Lightning Source LLC
Chambersburg PA
CBHW060245050426
42448CB00009B/1579